Are Black men doomed?

Debating Race series

David Theo Goldberg, *Are we all postracial yet?*
Ghassan Hage, *Is racism an environmental threat?*
Jonathan Marks, *Is science racist?*
Alford A. Young, Jr., *Are Black men doomed?*

Are Black men doomed?

ALFORD A. YOUNG, JR.

polity

First published in 2018 by Polity Press

Polity Press
65 Bridge Street
Cambridge CB2 1UR, UK

Polity Press
101 Station Landing
Suite 300
Medord, MA 02155, USA

ISBN-13: 978-1-5095-2205-7
ISBN-13: 978-1-5095-2206-4(pb)

A catalogue record for this book is available from the British Library.

Library of Congress Cataloging-in-Publication Data

Names: Young, Alford A., author.
Title: Are black men doomed? / Alford A. Young, Jr.
Description: Cambridge : Polity Press, 2017. | Series: Debating race | Includes bibliographical references and index.
Identifiers: LCCN 2017025319 (print) | LCCN 2017026080 (ebook) | ISBN 9781509522088 (Mobi) | ISBN 9781509522095 (Epub) | ISBN 9781509522057 (hardback) | ISBN 9781509522064 (pbk.)
Subjects: LCSH: African American men. | Stereotypes (Social psychology) | Identity (Psychology) | United States–Social conditions. | United States–Race relations.
Classification: LCC E185.86 (ebook) | LCC E185.86 .Y66 2017 (print) | DDC 907.2/02–dc23
LC record available at https://lccn.loc.gov/2017025319

Typeset in 11 on 15 pt Adobe Garamond
by Toppan Best-set Premedia Limited
Printed and bound in the UK by Clays Ltd, St Ives plc

For further information on Polity, visit our website:
politybooks.com

CONTENTS

The crisis of African American men and masculinity seems to have been around forever. It surely has been a point of concern in the United States for the past 30 years. It was three decades ago when these individuals began to garner extreme attention in the media and in policy discussions. Indeed, the precarious status of Black males became a high point of concern in the US conversation about the state and fate of African Americans in the post-civil rights era.

The problems that Black men face seemingly cover vast terrain. They exist in employment, education, physical and mental health and well-being, fatherhood and family relations, incarceration, surveillance, and detention at the hands of legal authorities, and in the myriad challenges and threats to their ability to construct a positive social identity and self-concept. Irrespective of how the general problem of African American men and masculinity is construed, however, the greatest dimension of their problem is that much of the public attention on them calls for what they must do to change themselves.

Consequently, even those professing to be empathetic to Black men often emphasize the material resources that they must acquire from more privileged others in order to enact such changes. This condition masks the deeper problem for African American men: the inability of others in US society to realize that an improved situation for African American men is contingent upon those others being willing to change, themselves. For the past 30 years, then, Black males have been framed as a problem in the US. The resolution of their plight, however, requires more thorough attention to the ways in which the US is a problem for them.

Transforming the situation of Black males requires more their changing themselves. The outcome of a more positive public identity and life situation for Black males cannot be achieved without some change in the public that has consistently framed them so problematically. Undoubtedly, there is no shortage of African American males who must change. Yet, a great deal must change around them in order for them to improve their life prospects and personal well-being. Essentially, what must change if Black men are to prevail in the modern world is the public perception of them. That is, others must learn to understand and accept that many of the standard portraits of these men and boys are incomplete if not inaccurate. Black men are framed as menacing and incorrigible. They are too often seen as uncompromisingly committed to themselves and to social destruction. Consequently, they are regarded as necessarily requiring social control and containment. As is well understood, the latter is achieved via incarceration or the kinds of surveillance provided by penal, policing, and other state institutions.

The following pages argue that a new conception of these men is in order. They make a case that a more thorough sense of who they are and what their capacities as citizens of the modern world happen to be are prematurely and severely handicapped by the contemporary misreading of them. All this is to say that Black men are doomed in US society, but they should not have to be. Indeed, they can prevail. However, they cannot do so without wholesale changes in the prevailing societal notions about them.

* * * * *

The situation of Black males in the US has been on my mind for quite some time. It has been for much of the same three decades in which the public has acknowledged a crisis. Unlike many Americans, however, they have been on my mind not because I am bothered by or fearful of them. Instead, I have been intrigued by them, but more importantly, I have been intrigued by the broader public response to them. The latter includes a measure of frustration with the public reading of these males. Yet I come to this constituency – which is one in which I hold membership – with a perspective rooted in hope and possibility as much as in recognizing the dire straits such men are in, and the role they sometimes play in putting themselves there. From a personal as well as an intellectual perspective, I find much to appreciate about Black males and much to consider about why others feel about them as they do. In fact, I have spent the past 20 years as a sociologist immersed in deep thought about whether the US can ever come to terms with Black men.

I am an African American male who was born and raised in the East Harlem section of New York City. Although mostly comprised of Hispanics, that community brought me into contact with a plethora of low-income African American males. My experiences there ultimately cemented my research focus and agenda. My late father was a college graduate and a Certified Public Accountant. My late mother worked as a legal secretary for much of my childhood. Although I lived in a highly impoverished urban neighborhood, I was not in any way as resource-challenged as most of my peers. Indeed, I was among the first children that I knew of from my neighborhood to leave it in order to attend (and actually help integrate) a Catholic elementary school in the considerably more elite mid-town section of Manhattan. Thereafter I attended Fordham Preparatory High School, a highly competitive Catholic school in the Bronx.

I first began to think seriously about how Black males in my community thought about their life situations and future prospects while a teenager. By my high-school years I noticed that most of the young men in my community were on a different, and much less promising trajectory. The recession of the late 1970s, the economic turbulence of the 1980s, and the crack epidemic that was occurring near the end of that decade appeared to be highly relevant to the stalled fortunes of these men, yet as an adolescent I did not possess the language and mindset that I now do to figure out what was going on. It simply appeared to me that over those decades more and more young men had become strung out and were without jobs.

When not focused on the plight of the people in my neighborhood, my father's professional networks enabled me to meet politicians, business executives, and other high-profile people that were in his social circles. Accordingly, as a young man I had constant and intimate exposure to people in poverty and in privilege. That resulted in vivid exposure to stratification, inequality, and social difference throughout my life. I interacted with many people at each end of and all along the socio-economic class continuum. I noticed that those at each end would rarely engage each other. I also noticed and was fascinated by the differences and similarities in their social outlooks and worldviews.

I came of age in the 1980s. That was the decade of my adolescence and early adulthood. It was when I decided to commit to the study of African American men as a life pursuit. It also was the period of the rise and sedimentation of the so-called underclass in the minds of the general public about the most disadvantaged residents of urban America. During that time it seemed like attitudes and opinions about Black men proliferated faster than did public interest in personal computers. Young Black males in urban communities were regarded in the media as a social menace. For many, the peak of public panic in that decade occurred near its end.

Media accounts reported that on the evening of April 19, 1989, close to 30 Black and Hispanic young men accosted, threatened, robbed, or assaulted people in the vicinity of the northeast corner of New York City's Central Park (the portion of the park adjacent to East Harlem) (Burns 2011). In a wooded area in that section of the park the horrifically abused body of a female jogger was found, apparently left for dead. The report of that discovery created a moment of panic about the consequences of urban living in the US (Burns 2011).

Four Black and one Hispanic adolescent males were convicted of assault, robbery, riot, rape, sexual abuse, and attempted murder in association with the discovery. They were crucified in the media and in public conversation (Burns 2011). Edward I. Koch, the mayor of the City of New York, Mario Cuomo, the Governor of the State of New York, and various civic leaders and politicians called for the condemnation of these boys. Ultimately, they were convicted and spent between six and 13 years in prison.

The convictions were vacated in 2002 due to the confession of Matias Reyes, a man who was not associated with those originally convicted. A re-investigation of the crime resulted in the uncovering of police misconduct, including the collection of questionable evidence used against these boys to convict them. That discovery was publicized far too late to counter-balance the intensity by which urban-based Black males in 1989 were deemed a threat to the public well-being.

Apparently, a lot of bad behavior went on during the night of April 19, 1989. However, what also went on that night was the vilification of innocent boys. Alongside this vilification was the validation of the extreme indictment of Black males in urban America. The concept of wilding – a description of the presumed uncontrollable and extreme conduct of males of color in the streets of urban America – was introduced in the media to define the seeming lawlessness of these individuals (Burns 2011).

Also unfolding in the 1980s was the New York City Police Department's introduction of neighborhood sweeps to counter the crack epidemic. The efforts resembled military operations designed to capture fugitives. Except, in this case, people occupying street corners that were deemed to be drug distribution sites were picked up en masse by the police in night-time sweeps. The result was that by the 1990s low-income, urban-based Black men were firmly constituted in the public eye as being in trouble, riddled with personal problems, and troublesome for nearly everybody else.

Having grown up in East Harlem, and having been around the kind of men that were represented as such, I believed there was much more to them than this negative imagery conveyed. Since the mid-1990s, I have conducted research that has put my research teams and me into contact with nearly 500 Black males, most of whom could be categorized as exemplifying that crisis. In the course of my studies I have discovered that these individuals were more than just men with problems or who brought problems to others. They also were men with possibility and potential. I learned that they have not necessarily given up on themselves even if they made some difficult and sometimes tragic choices.

It was my deep intrigue into how these men made sense of their life situations that motivated me to pursue a research agenda on low-income African Americans. As a sociologist, my project has been to document what Black men think about themselves and the social worlds in which they live (Young 2000, 2004, 2006, 2007, 2016). I also explored what they say about aspects of the world that they have not experienced, including the everyday world of work and work opportunity, and what they understand to be stable and desirable family living.

My goal, in essence, was to explore the humanity of people that, like my peers in East Harlem, were too easily depicted as flawed or maladjusted, rather than thoughtful, contemplative, and complex. The lingering question for me, and one that is central to every research endeavor that I ever pursued, was how do African Americans think about themselves, and how does that compare with how others think about them? Even as I go about doing research today, nearly two decades after moving away from East Harlem, I still contemplate how the men of my neighborhood might respond to the questions that I ask in the field.

In the following pages I affirm that Black men have been doomed. Accordingly, any effort for recovery necessarily involves constituencies external to them. Their capacity to prevail involves as much action on our part as on theirs. A part of our societal challenge, then, is to re-educate ourselves about Black males. That being said, the argument here is to confront and challenge the idea that pathology is foundational to who Black men are and what Black masculinity is, especially when focused on low-income men.

It is possible for the general public in the US to be more understanding of them, if not grow to appreciate them more fully. However, the path toward that end is not linear. The possibility for this to occur has more to do with how others think about Black men than how they, themselves, behave or engage the social world. That is, the ability to embrace Black men, or at least divorce them from doom in the US, is rooted in the capacity for others to understand where, when, and how these men share in the social world as much as all others who constitute modern society. Until there is greater capacity to identify with and better understand these men, they will continue to be damned.

The proposed project of understanding and identification is two-fold. It includes both rethinking the collective sentiment about these men as well as taking more thorough account of how these men think and feel about themselves. The following pages are intended to encourage both efforts. I make this case by drawing from research on these men, what I have observed about how others respond to and portray them, and what I have experienced as one of them.

In making this case I am aware that some may regard the following commentary as one-sided. My manner of immersing myself into the lives of nearly 500 such men for research purposes may convey that I aspire to detract attention from their flaws so that I can use their words solely to paint them as wholly positive individuals. Some may be steadfast in discerning that Black men who have been in trouble with the law, with their families, or with other people simply do not take accountability for their actions. Accordingly, the ensuing logic implies, why accept the claim that others must become more accountable to them? To be clear, I do not mean to deny all of the negatives associated with at least some Black men. That which Black men have done that is detrimental to themselves and to others has been thoroughly documented in media and other public venues. Therefore, neither erasure nor denial of that could ever be a plausible objective. Nor can the objective be to erase or deny that some of these men have substantial work to do on their own behalf. Instead, my quest is to offer new portraits of such men, because while some have long ago recognized these men in the ways I suggest (especially those more intimately connected to such men), those portraits have not surfaced in the broader popular imagination. Consequently, the objective at hand is to assert and affirm that if any of us aim to better understand who Black men are and what they might become in society, the less recognized dimensions of their lives underlying these new portraits merit attention.

* * * * *

I wish to thank Emma Longstaff, who initially invited me to consider submitting a book for the Debating Race series at Polity Press. I am not clear what she saw in me that compelled her to ask me to do something very different from the kind of writing I've been doing as a sociologist, but I am glad that she did. Shortly after informing her that I was willing to take a stab at doing so, Jonathan Skerrett assumed the position of editor. He guided me from early drafts to a finished product. Jonathan served as my distant audience – the very kind of person at whom this book is targeted. He was conscientious and sensitive about the topic, but was removed enough from it that he would raise questions that encouraged me to offer more substantive explanations and more precise clarifications. The Polity Press team, including Clare Ansell and Ian Tuttle, were vital for allowing this book to come into fruition.

I appreciate the support of William Julius Wilson and Sudhir Venkatesh, two of the people who have greatly informed my thinking about Black men in America; as well as my spouse, Carla O'Connor, the woman who has been most influential in affecting my thinking about such men. I am hopeful that this work can lead to a better world for all Black men, especially for Alford III and Kai, the two Black males for whom I am responsible in guiding and serving. Finally, this is for all the Black men whom I have researched and whom I have known. My sharing in their lives in whatever way I have has caused me to hold onto so much in the back of my head; things that I have not ever put in the public space. The publication of this book means that I've now been able to do so.

ONE

The problem with Black males

I met "Blue" one day about 20 years ago, in the living room of the apartment that I shared with my fiancée. At the time we were pursuing our graduate studies at the University of Chicago. Blue was a laborer hired by the movers whose services I secured to transfer our belongings to western Massachusetts. Our move to Northampton, Massachusetts would allow my fiancée and me to spend our final year of graduate study on fellowships at neighboring liberal arts colleges in that region (at Smith College and Hampshire College, respectively). Blue was an African American male who appeared to me to be in his mid-thirties. At first sight, not much was particularly distinctive about him. I could not know it at the time, but the story Blue told me would become one of my signature testimonies of the ultimate possibility for Black men in the United States.

The husband and wife team that the moving company sent to us brought along Blue to help with packing and loading on the front end of the move (Massachusetts-based help would unload at the back end). At close to six feet in height, Blue was not very stocky yet he was solidly built and seemed quite capable of doing his job. My fiancée and I observed the moving team pick up various items, maneuver them to the elevator, and then down to the truck. Blue seemed especially focused on moving our bookshelves and office furniture, which was an especially relevant skill set given that my fiancée and I had acquired much of such material over the course of our six years of graduate study.

At some point during their work I overheard the husband tell Blue that he seemed to really know how to handle office furniture. He responded that office moving was his specialty. "I know how to do office," is how he explained himself. Having never before hired, much less even observed professional movers in action, I found myself drawn to the manner in which Blue worked. He positioned file cabinets at particular angles prior to moving them, and he tilted bookcases in ways that made them seem especially maneuverable. He seemed to work hard at making moving look easy.

At about mid-afternoon the team took a break for lunch. Blue grabbed a sandwich and a drink out of a paper bag and sat on the floor of my now semi-bare living room. Having heard much of Blue's conversations with the moving team throughout the morning, I knew he was from the south side of Chicago, a residential area almost exclusively occupied by low-income African Americans who were struggling to achieve the American Dream. Having ventured into that part of town for research purposes, I knew that Blue was from a community where many Black men in particular found their way into illicit activities, as well as into the gangs that regulated them. I was keenly interested in this man who had what I regarded as a unique job and who was from an area of the city that had no shortage of African American males without jobs of any sort.

I plopped down next to Blue while he was eating and asked him how he found his way into the moving business. In between bites of his sandwich Blue told me his story. He said, "When I was younger I was a very bad boy." He told me how he was involved in gangs and the traditional activities that gangs in Chicago immersed themselves in. Blue sold drugs. He stole merchandise. He helped plan and participate in attacks on rival gang members. In short, he represented the kind of public menace that appears in the minds of many people when they think of what is wrong with Black men.

He explained that his commitment to a wayward path was interrupted by his uncle. One day when Blue was in his late-teens his uncle told him that he needed to get out of the streets or the streets would take control of him. In order to make this happen his uncle told him to pack his bag. Blue was going to be traveling with him for a few weeks. Blue told me that he knew that his uncle drove a truck for a living, but he did not know much else about what he did.

Blue packed his bag and joined his uncle. He soon found out that the travel would first involve helping his uncle load up a truck full of household goods from a small home in Chicago. Once the truck was loaded, Blue hopped in and his uncle drove the two of them to Florida with the material in tow. Blue told me that this was his first trip outside of the city of Chicago.

"I saw green grass and trees and fields," he told me. "And I saw small towns that did not have lots of people in them." He also said, "I saw places where Black and White kids played together, and everybody seemed to be having fun." He said, "It all was so different from Chicago." His manner of speaking made it almost feel like he was telling a fairy tale.

After they arrived in Florida, Blue helped his uncle unload the truck at a small house there. When they were done Blue asked his uncle, "What are we going to do now?" His uncle told him, "We are going to go someplace else, pick up some more stuff, and take it somewhere else." That was Blue's introduction to professional moving. Indeed, it was his first experience with formal work. As importantly, it was Blue's first-hand exposure to social worlds far beyond and very different from inner-city Chicago.

I have thought about Blue quite often since hearing his story more than two decades ago. The move he made from unemployed gang member seemingly locked into a closed world on the south side of Chicago to a man who encountered parts of the United States that severely contrasted with what he experienced in his Chicago neighborhood. Among many other factors (the social support provided by his uncle not an insignificant one), this exposure allowed him to reconstruct a vision of himself, his social world, and his potential place within it.

When I met him he was by no means financially secure, but he was secure about knowing what he could do with himself and what he wanted to do in the future. He wanted to own his own truck. This would enable him to have control of his involvement in professional moving. He told me that he was several years away from making this happen, but he had mapped out a plan for securing his future. The first part of the plan was demonstrating his indispensability as a packer and loader so that he could establish an identity as a good employee. The plan also included saving money to invest in a small truck.

At first sight, I had no idea that Blue was a former gang member who lived his teenage years quite unfocused on his future. Instead, I saw a man who knew how to get his job done, and his abilities greatly impressed the people that hired him for that day. He also knew what so many of the near 500 men that I have interviewed in the course of my research on low-income, urban-based Black men did not know, which is what parts of the world look and feel like that are far removed from the kind of disadvantaged communities where many struggling Black people reside.

More than 20 years have passed since my conversation with Blue. Since that time, I have continued to wonder what capacity many Americans have to imagine how someone like Blue became the person that he did given the life he led since his youth. What capacity, I question, do they have to envision any socio-economically disadvantaged Black man as a potentially positive individual?

Not every Black man living in socio-economic constraint can benefit from an uncle capable of delivering the kind of opportunities that Blue's could. Yet, the importance of Blue's story is not simply that his uncle, another Black man, acted on his behalf. It is also that Blue acted on his own behalf to learn and plan a future for himself given what his uncle had exposed him to. The importance of Blue's story can be lost if framed solely as a heroic tale of moving from desperate living to the verge of possible stability if not wholesale success. His story accounts for how a Black man can typify the crisis of Black men when viewed from one vantage point, but who appears to be wholly capable of serving himself and serving others when viewed from the vantage point of my living room.

The kind of man that Blue was in his adolescence and early adult years was the kind that I have consistently studied over the past two decades. The kind of man that Blue became by the time that I met him exemplified my hopes for the men that I have studied. In the same way that I could not see his past without him telling me all about it, Americans often do not see new possibilities for Black men because of what they witness and interpret about their present condition. Admittedly, seeing new possibilities is not easy. Creating such a vision, however, first means taking careful account of the present-day realities for these men. This must be done not to cement preconceived notions about them, but rather as a precondition for imagining them differently.

* * * * *

Long-standing preconceived notions about Black men have not emerged in a vacuum. Instead, this problematic portrait is tied to various social outcomes and processes, and these should not be ignored. They concern the health, employment, and educational status of these individuals. A quick overview of this landscape is necessary in order to demonstrate precisely what these men must work against, and what the rest of us must realize and consider, in the quest for them to be regarded in a better light.

In 2015 *The New York Times* published an article indicating that more than 1.5 million Black men in the US were missing (Wolfers et al. 2015). The article was not about mass-scale abduction, but rather about the removal of these men from residential communities and workplaces. To be exact, their disappearance was due to premature mortality (approximately 900,000 men) and incarceration (in the region of 625,000 men). Consequently, for every 100 Black women not in jail, there were only 83 available Black men, or 17 missing Black men for every 100 Black women. The authors of this report also stated that among White Americans there is only one missing man for every 100 women. The case of missing Black men triggers attention to various measures and indicators of the problem with Black males.

Men in general, but certainly Black males, account for their sense of manhood by their ability to perform as family providers, husbands, fathers, employees, and community members (Hammond and Mattis 2005). However, a litany of social scientific and other research has given credence to the notion that a crisis for Black men abounds, and their invisibility or nominal presence in many spheres of social life has been well documented. The statistics do tell a compelling story. The first story to report is exactly who constitutes the population of Black men in the US (see table 1.1).

According to census data, the Black male population in the United States makes up 48% of the total Black population. Black males are on average younger than other males in the United States (31 years old compared to 36 years old for "all males"). The higher mortality rate than males on average means that the percentage of the population who are males declines much more quickly for Black males as they get older.

Table 1.1 Black men, population at a glance

	Black men	**All men**
Population	21.5 million	151.7 million
Median age	31	36
Percent compared to females		
Under 18 years of age	48%	49%
18 to 34	51%	51%
35 to 64	47%	49%
65 and older	40%	44%

Source: BlackDemographics.com, 2013.

Health and physical well-being

In 2006, the homicide death rate for young African American men was 84.6 per 100,000 of the population compared with 5 per 100,000 of the population for young White men. While homicide death rates decline for older African American men, the rates among African American men aged 25–44 are still disturbingly high (61 per 100,000 of the population) when compared with Whites of that age group (5.1 per 100,000 of the population) (Kaiser Family Foundation 2006). In 2006 it was found that Black males aged 15–19 die from homicide at 46 times the rate of their White counterparts (National Urban League 2007). As table 1.2 indicates, in the years to follow, reports of the health and well-being of Black males did not improve.

Other measures of health and well-being for African American men are equally disturbing. In February 2016, the Centers for Disease Control and Prevention (CDC) released a report assessing the lifetime risk of HIV in the United States. The report revealed that for heterosexual Black men in the US there was a 1 in 20 lifetime risk for human immunodeficiency virus (HIV) (compared to a 1 in 132 lifetime risk for White heterosexual men) (Centers for Disease Control and Prevention 2016). Black men are similarly disproportionately affected by the HIV/acquired immune deficiency syndrome (AIDS) pandemic when compared to other population groups. Black men have more than seven times the AIDS rate of non-Hispanic White men. In addition, Black men are more than nine times more likely to die from HIV/AIDS than White men (Office of Minority Health 2008).

Furthermore, African American men have the lowest life expectancy and highest mortality rate among men and women in all other racial or ethnic groups in the United States. The life expectancy at birth is 70 years for Black men compared with 76 years for White men, 76 years for Black women, and 81 years for White women (National Center for Health Statistics 2007). The mortality rate for African American men is 1.3 times that of White men, 1.7 times that of American Indian/Alaska Native men, 1.8 times that of Hispanic men, and 2.4 times that of Asian or Pacific Islander men (Kaiser Family Foundation 2006).

Black men are 30% more likely to die from heart disease as compared with White men. The mortality rate for diabetes for Black men is 51.7 per 100,000 as compared to 25.6 per 100,000 for their White male counterparts (Xanthos et al. 2010). They also are 37% more likely than White men to develop lung cancer. Between 2000 and 2003, Black men had an age-adjusted lung cancer death rate that was 32% higher than that for White men (death rates of 97.2 versus 73.4 per

Table 1.2 Causes of deaths for Black and White males (%) (based on top 10 ranking, 2014)

	15-19 years old		20-24 years old		25-34 years old	
	Black	**White**	**Black**	**White**	**Black**	**White**
Assault homicide	**48.3**	7.6	**47.5**	7.1	**31.8**	5.1
Suicide	7.1	**24.8**	9.7	**21.3**	7.2	**18.2**
Malignant neoplasms (cancer)	3.8	**5.7**	2.9	**4.5**	3.9	**5.8**
Heart disease	**3.5**	2.5	**3.3**	2.8	**9.5**	6.2
Hypertension	**0.5**	0.4	Not in top 10	**0.5**	**1.4**	0.9
Diabetes	Not in top 10	**0.3**	**0.8**	0.6	**2.0**	1.1
HIV/AIDS	Not in top 10	Not in top 10	**1.4**	Not in top 10	**3.8**	Not in top 10

Source: Centers for Disease Control and Prevention, 2016.

35-44 years old		45-54 years old		55-64 years old		65 years and over	
Black	**White**	**Black**	**White**	**Black**	**White**	**Black**	**White**
12.8	2.8	**3.3**	Not in top 10	Not in top 10	Not in top 10	Not in top 10	Not in top 10
4.3	**13.4**	Not in top 10	**7.0**	Not in top 10	**3.1**	Not in top 10	Not in top 10
9.3	**11.3**	19.2	**20.9**	28.0	**30.4**	25.8	24.1
20.9	14.8	**26.7**	22.0	**26.4**	24.1	26.7	**26.8**
3.7	1.9	**4.4**	2.4	**4.9**	2.8	**6.0**	4.8
3.7	2.5	**4.6**	3.3	**4.6**	3.7	**4.5**	2.9
4.5	1.2	**4.0**	Not in top 10	**2.0**	Not in top 10	Not in top 10	Not in top 10

100,000, respectively) (American Lung Association 2007). Finally, in the 30–39 age group, Black men are about 14 times more likely to develop kidney failure due to hypertension than White men (US Renal Data System 2005), and Black men are 60% more likely to die from a stroke than their White adult counterparts (Office of Minority Health 2008).

Some of these data reflect the problematic ways in which Black men manage their health. Research has demonstrated that they are more likely than others to have undiagnosed and/or poorly managed chronic conditions such as diabetes, cancer, and heart disease (Warner and Hayward 2006; Williams 2003). Moreover, Black men, irrespective of their income level, are 50% less likely than White men to have had contact with physicians during the past year (Hammond et al. 2011).

Employment

African American males aged 16–64 had a lower participation rate in the labor force (67%) compared to "all males" (80%) (see table 1.3). Labor force participation refers to the percentage of men who were either working or looking for work. Males not in the labor force include those who may be full-time students, disabled, and others

Table 1.3 Earnings and employment

	Black men	**All men**
Ages 16 to 64		
Percent who are in the labor force	67	80
Percent who are unemployed	11.2	7.3
Percent who are below the poverty line	26	15
Ages 16 and up		
Median earnings for 2013	$37,290	$48,099
Percent who worked full-time, year-round	37	48
Percent of earnings NOT from full-time work	23	23
Percent who had no earnings all year	40	30
Occupation type (%)		
White collar	42	75
Blue collar	26	17
Service occupations	23	8

Source: BlackDemographics.com, 2013.

who are not looking or gave up looking for employment for other reasons.

The 37% of African American males who worked full time all year in 2013 had median earnings of $37,290 compared to $48,099 for "all men." Of Black males aged 16–64, 40% had no earnings in 2013. This was higher than the 30% with no earnings of "all men" in the same age group. Also a larger percentage of Black males aged 16–64 were unemployed than "all men" and were living below the poverty line (26%) than "all men" (15%). Compared to "all men" in the United States, Black men who worked were much less likely to work in occupations that are considered white collar and were much more likely to hold blue-collar or service jobs. Only 42% of working Black men held white-collar jobs compared to 75% of "all men."

Education

The greatest disparity between Black men and "all men" in the US is between those who have and those who do not have a bachelor's degree. Only 17% of Black men have a bachelor's degree compared to 30% of "all men" (see table 1.4). Second is the number of Black men who finished high school but did not pursue higher education (35% compared to 28%). While only 18% of Black men more than 25 did not complete high school, their percentage is higher than the percentage for men of all races and ethnic groups together. Other trends and

Table 1.4 Highest level of educational attainment (age 25 and above, %)

	Black men	**All men**
Less than high-school diploma	18	14
High-school graduate (or GED)	35	28
Some college, no degree	24	21
Associate's degree	7	7
Bachelor's degree or higher	17	30
Attended college	48	69

Source: BlackDemographics.com, 2013.

statistics indicate the severity of the condition of Black males and educational attainment:

- According to 2012–2013 estimates of high-school graduation rates, 59% of Black men graduated from high school in comparison to 80% of White males who did so.
- These estimates reflect a 21 percentage point gap on the Black–White male high-school graduation rate.
- In 2009–2010 there was a 19 percentage point gap (Schott Foundation for Public Education 2015).

Table 1.5 Percentage of boys at or above proficiency by grade and subject, 2013

	4th grade **Mathematics**	8th grade **Mathematics**	4th grade **Reading**	8th grade **Reading**
White	55%	45%	41%	38%
Black	18%	13%	14%	12%

Source: Institute of Education Sciences, 2013.

Problems abound for Black boys prior to the post-secondary experience. A recent report indicates that no more than 18% of Black boys perform at or above proficiency in reading and mathematics in the 4th and 8th grades, while no fewer than 38% of White boys perform at or above proficiency in the same categories (see table 1.5).

Incarceration

Of adults in 2001 who had ever served time in prison, nearly as many were Black males (2,166,000) as White (2,203,000), and this is out of a population of more than 20 million Black men in comparison to nearly 150 million White males. At that time, the rate of ever having gone to prison among adult Black males (16.6%) was more than six times as high as among adult White males (2.6%). An estimated 22% of Black males aged 35–44 in 2001 had at some point been confined in State or Federal prison, compared to 3.5% of White males in the same age group. Finally, as of 2001, about one in three Black males and one in seventeen White males are expected to go to prison during their lifetime, if current incarceration rates remain unchanged (The Sentencing Project 2013).

Over time the condition for Black males has not improved. In 2006 there were 1,502,200 male sentenced prisoners under State or Federal jurisdiction. Of these, 478,000 were White American males, representing 31.8% of the incarcerated population, and 534,200 were Black American males, representing 35.6% of the incarcerated population (The Sentencing Project 2013) – remembering, of course, the much greater number of White males than Black males in the general population.

The story is not dramatically better as we turn to contemporary data. In 2010 about 6% of Black men aged 18–64 were in State or Federal prison, or in a municipal jail. This is three times higher than the 2% of "all men" in the same age group. Moreover, approximately 34% of all working-age Black men who are not incarcerated are ex-offenders. This compared to 12% of "all men"

Table 1.6 Number and percentage of prisoners sentenced under the jurisdiction of State or Federal correctional authorities

	Number	**Percent**
All males	1,371,879	(100)
White males	446,700	32.5
Black males	501,300	36.5
Hispanic males	301,500	21.9

Source: Bureau of Justice Statistics 2015, and author's own calculations.

who have at some point in their lives been convicted of a felony (Bureau of Justice Statistics 2010; Center for Economic and Policy Research 2010).

Finally, a recent report indicates that Black men constitute the largest percentage of men sentenced under the jurisdiction of State and Federal correctional authorities (36.5%) even as they constitute only approximately 15% of the male population in the United States (see table 1.6).

Fatherhood

In recent decades, high rates of unemployment, drug sentencing policies, and increased policing in urban centers have been linked to Black men's increased and disproportionate incarceration (Goffman 2014; Western and Wildeman 2009). Higher incarceration rates have led to many Black fathers rotating in and out of their children's lives. Their incarceration not only renders them physically unavailable but also limits their ability to offer financial and material provisions. The resulting strains to father–partner and father–child relationships result from the often unsatisfactory means by which family needs are fulfilled during fathers' imprisonment (Swisher and Waller 2008; Western and Wildeman 2009). Black unmarried fathers face the additional financial burden of arrears, defined as the accumulation of unpaid child support, during their incarceration. Upon release these fathers encounter sometimes insurmountable arrears in addition to the prospect of paying current and future child support (Holzer et al. 2005). Further, they are challenged to readjust to society, find a job, and reconnect with their families.

By 2012, 55.1% of all Black children, 31.1% of all Hispanic children, and 20.7% of all White children were living in single-parent homes (US Census Bureau 2012). This is an increase from 2010, where the percentage for Black children stood at 48.5, and 2000, where the percentage for these children was 51.1 (US Census Bureau 2012). While these data do not reveal the extent to which Black men engage their children and invest in quality time, as the great majority of single-parent households are female-headed, they do affirm the physical challenges that Black fathers confront in being present with their children on a regular, if not everyday, basis.

* * * * *

The statistics are stunning. They effectively convey that a crisis exists for Black males in the US. They inform about the quality of life that Black males are forced to live. Yet, they also serve to prevent other kinds of realizations about who these men are and what their capabilities happen to be. The statistics on health, employment, education, and family status easily imply that Black men have failed. Yet, other reports indicate how much society has failed them, in part because they appear to have fallen short in measures of social mobility and life satisfaction. In fact, most recently, the crisis of Black men has been made evident in public debate about whether they should be permitted to live. A rash of killings of African American males at the hands of police officers and citizens claiming to act in defense of their communities has been in the purview of the public for several years (and, in full disclosure, African American women have been subjected to this condition as well). As far as Black males are concerned, the deaths of Trayvon Martin, Michael Brown, Tamir Rice, Freddie Gray, and others have been well reported in the press (an overview of such reporting is found in Young 2017). What has also been reported, and what purports to be more troubling for Black men that are alive, is how much the presumed character of these men has been taken to be a justifiable factor in their deaths (Young 2017).

According to news sources, following coverage of his death at the hands of George Zimmerman, questions abounded as to whether Trayvon Martin was a marijuana user and a petty criminal, and whether his presumed status as such should serve as validating the circumstances of his death (Alcindor 2012; Alvarez 2013; Robles 2012). The killing of Michael Brown in Ferguson, Missouri, in August 2014 was followed by discussion of whether he was uncontrollable and threatening to those he encountered immediately prior to his being left to die on a street in that St. Louis suburb (Alcindor et al. 2014; Tacopino 2014). Tamir Rice was killed by a police officer in Cleveland on November 22, 2014, while in possession of a toy gun. The public image associated with him on that day was that of a Black male who appeared to be primed to do harm, even though other African American children and adults occupied the very public park near where he was killed and were unfazed by a Black boy in possession of a toy gun (Fitzsimmons 2014). Finally, at the time of his death on April

19, 2015, Freddie Gray was a 25-year-old ex-offender who was shackled and placed without a seat belt in a Baltimore City police van. In some of the media coverage of this event and the subsequent trial of the police officers indicted for Gray's death, he was referred to as the son of an illiterate heroin addict (Husband 2015).

Media coverage of the public debate following the death of these and other African American males centered on whether they conducted themselves as proper and decent people, or whether they appeared to be threatening or dangerous immediately prior to their deaths. In some cases, attention was devoted to whether they were substance abusers or delinquents. Underlying the conversations from those who defended or otherwise validated the actions of those who killed them was the image of Black males as badly behaved and threatening to other Americans. In short, what they did, who they were, or how they appeared to be at the time of their deaths was evidence enough to justify their deaths, or at least provide credible evidence as to why they occurred. The acquittals of US police officers initially charged with or investigated for the killing of African American males who were unarmed were grounded in arguments that those men posed extreme threat to the police officers who responded as they did to them – even though these men were neither armed nor in the midst of verbally threatening the police at the time of these occurrences (Abbasi 2017; Bouie 2017; Thrasher 2017). It is not simply the deaths of these Black males, but how they were accounted for in discussion of their deaths, that points to an additional dimension of the crisis of Black males. That crisis is the devaluation of the Black male body.

The past three decades have been a time in which media and technology have been indispensable tools for the proliferation of negative images of Black men and masculinity. These tools have allowed audiences to absorb these images without being in close contact with or proximity to these men. The troubling portrait of African American males has been sustained by a barrage of negative images about them emanating from mainstream and social media (an overview of such portraits is provided in Opportunity Agenda 2012). In these media, Black men are seen as highly predisposed to violence rather than conscientious, and easily given to surrender and withdrawal from schools and job prospects rather than of the media investigating whether poor schools and lower-tier jobs in their communities can actually serve them well. Messages from these outlets reify the negative public sentiment about Black males as unlawful, threatening, or unworthy.

Of course, that some of the Black males have done terrible things to themselves as well as to other people cannot be dismissed or denied. Research on low-income African American males has provided ample evidence that those who have ventured into these activities are conscious of what they have done and the societal impact that it has had (Harding 2010; Sullivan 1989; Venkatesh 2000, 2006; Williams 1989; Young 2004). However, the depiction of these males as having the capacity to be self-reflective or conscientious is suppressed by the pervasiveness of the character assassination. More concerning is the fact that African American males who do nothing to contribute to the negative public portrait of them suffer the consequences of this pervasive public portrait as they are assumed to be as problematic as those who effectively contribute to it. As sociologist Devah Pager and others have shown in researching the attitudes of employers, Black men are presumed to be ex-offenders or unworthy candidates for jobs even if no record of such a status appears on their resumes (Pager 2007; Pager et al. 2009a, 2009b; Quillian and Pager 2001; Wacquant 2001, 2005, 2010). Consequently, these males continue to be susceptible to a negative public identity that they in no way have helped to create and sustain.

This being the case, there is much work to be done to reconstitute the character of African American males. That work extends far beyond any superficial or short-sighted mandate for them to desist from engaging in problematic behavior. It also necessarily extends beyond the challenge of remediating the conduct of the police and other authority agents as they too often function with impunity in regard to Black males.

The crisis regarding the health and well-being of Black males, therefore, pertains not only to their already precarious physical condition. It also has to do with the rationalization and justification of the nefarious treatment of their bodies. Indeed, the inability to live healthy lives is not all there is to the contemporary crisis for Black males. It also includes the inability to be accorded dignity in death. Consequently, a present-day condition of the crisis of Black males is that the literal assassination of the Black male body is now coupled with a thorough character assassination. That is, if Black men are not subjected to violence at the hands of law enforcement authorities or everyday citizens, they are subjected to persecution that limits their prospects even if they possess the necessary credentials or experience for what they desire to pursue. Such men are boxed in by a publicly accepted script that assigns them an unworthy status. The enforcement of this script is necessarily a project for others to confront and challenge, and this means that the public must radically turn to addressing *its* problem with Black males rather than solely focusing on their problems.

TWO

Our problem with Black males

The problem with Black men is far from just their own problem. It is as much a societal one. It is *our* problem as much as it is *theirs*. Our problem with Black males rests in a public portrait of them that lacks appropriate depth and complexity. Many such men have the resolve to function in ways that contrast with the imagery associated with them. However, these men are too often perceived to be invested in delinquency and indecency. They are too often seen as hopeless. They are too often regarded as profligate and incorrigible. They are not believed to be capable of grasping new and better possibilities for themselves, or even maintaining the desire to do so. The societal default mentality is that these men should be given up on precisely because they have already given up on themselves. Indeed, our problem with Black males is as old as the crisis.

The contemporary image of Black males that the US has embraced is rooted in the emergence of the age of the underclass. Starting in the early 1980s, the concept of underclass gained purchase as a mechanism for labeling socio-economically marginalized, urban-based people of color. The term was initially used in social-scientific inquiry and policy circles at that time to designate a segment of the urban poor as a criminally inclined, violence-prone, and culturally deficient group of individuals who were locked in an inescapable web of economic deprivation and pathology. The underclass was made up of the most immobile and socially isolated of these urban dwellers. They had the fewest prospects for upward mobility and they experienced little sustained interaction with those in more mobile positions. Hence, they were understood to be the most immobile and socially isolated of the urban poor (Aponte 1990; Wilson 1987).

The underclass became a lightning-rod concept for generating public attention to the urban poor, and not necessarily in an ultimately constructive manner. In essence, this term was used as an identifier of behavior and public demeanor (Anderson 1989, 1990, 1999; Auletta 1982; Billson 1996; Bourgois 1995; Majors and Billson 1992). Public beliefs about their moral and cultural shortcomings helped to engineer a warped vision not only of their capacities for positive individual and collective action, but of their very public identities. Hence, it is not simply what these individuals do as societal actors, but who they are that constitutes their problematic status.

The very image of the Black male body often conjures up indictment. It is that effect that undergirds the problem that society has with Black men. An initial step toward addressing this problem is unpacking how such a strong culture of indictment came into being for Black men. This is the business of this chapter.

* * * * *

The backdrop for scholarly and public emphasis on the perniciousness of the urban underclass is the public space in which these men seem to predominate, more commonly referred to as "the streets." Black men appear to be so thoroughly situated in the American public mindset as street-oriented people. This orientation is not taken as positive. The streets that these men occupy are regarded as dangerous and unfitting for "mainstream" people. Consequently, the streets, themselves, occupy a place of importance in discussions of the fate of Black men (Anderson 1999) as the backdrop for the danger and perniciousness associated with them.

Several decades ago, sociologist Lee Rainwater (1970) became one of the first social scientists to draw attention to turbulent and unsafe streets as a primary characteristic of low-income urban communities and the people who live in them. He did so by extrapolating on what he described as the anomic street culture of urban America, which resulted from economic disinvestment and physical decay in the urban communities populated by disadvantaged marginalized people. Anomie referred to the lack of safety, security, and comfort in the public spaces that comprised urban, low-income African American communities. Rainwater's classic work, *Behind Ghetto Walls: Black Families in a Federal Slum* (1970), was based on a study of family dynamics of residents in the Pruitt-Igoe public housing development in St. Louis. As he saw it, residents of these communities experienced little collective trust and security as a result of living and interacting with one another amidst despair and blight. He also discussed how the streets were the structural contexts whereby violence, threats, challenges, and insecurities were managed, disguised, or otherwise surfaced as causal factors for at least some of the profligate public behaviors that ultimately emerged in people's lives.

Rainwater argued that low-income Black Americans embraced unique cultural orientations and practices precisely because of the structural constraints they faced. The emerging image was the prototypical *strong* Black man, perhaps best exemplified contemporarily by any number of now legendary gangster rap artists such as the members of NWA, 50 Cent, Tupac Shakur, Notorious BIG, or Ice-T. Humility, indecisiveness, and timidity were suppressed by images of aggression and intensity.

The streets were where these representations were demonstrated and made observable to others.

The street also was a focal point for Elliot Liebow in his classic work, *Tally's Corner: A Study of Negro Street-corner Men* (1967). Liebow argued that public spaces, and especially the street corner, provided a place for disadvantaged Black men to demonstrate and promote their moral worth to others. The street corner was a relevant platform for such demonstrations because its inhabitants had no secure access to employment sectors or highly regarded social statuses that could otherwise affirm their moral worth.

Liebow showed how feelings of defeat and deficiency are managed on the street corner as the men do things to elevate their public image among their peers (e.g., animated interaction with their children, for whom they otherwise cannot provide much material support) and reduce the emotional turmoil in their lives. He argued that much of what these men did on the street corner helped them to present a positive public persona as compensation for the personal and family-based problems they encountered. This argument about the utility of the street corner or engineering social conduct brought forth an additional perspective to Rainwater's discussion of the anomic quality of the streets in low-income urban areas. Both demonstrated the relevance of public space in the lives of Black American men. Yet, both also drew attention to the ways in which public space was related to some problematic aspects of their lives.

Rainwater, Liebow, and others foreshadowed the ways in which the streets would surface in the latter third of the twentieth century as sites of concern and consternation in the lives of low-income, urban-based African American men. More recent scholarship on socio-economic disadvantage in urban communities revitalized and amplified the idea that there is little safe public space for African Americans in the inner cities of the US by emphasizing the rise in violence and criminal activity in urban America that was a by-product of the underclass era (Anderson 1989, 1990; Bourgois 1995; Venkatesh 2000; Young 2004). During the 1980s, a period of sweeping public exposure to, and rapid acceptance of, the concept of the underclass, an amplified vision of the danger of the streets, and the dangerousness of their occupants – most often Black men – came to the surface. Accordingly, a consequence of the debate about the existence of an entrenched underclass in urban America was the forwarding of a lucid portrait of the urban terrain itself as especially dangerous, hostile, and uninviting.

The spaces Black men were forced to inhabit had a direct impact on the social identities they could assume. The kind of self-affirmation that unfolded as available to them was in response to the tumultuousness of disadvantaged communities. It provided a means for Black men to save face in social space. The kind of bravado unfolding on basketball courts, in barbershops, or on street corners as men lived their lives has been argued by some to reflect self-preservation efforts by these men (Anderson 1990, 1999; Billson 1996; Liebow 1967; Majors and Billson 1992). Indeed, the social spaces that such men occupy often demand that they maintain aggressive dispositions so that they can manage the challenges that these communities present. The needs and demands for professing bravado, intensity, and assertiveness while engaging public spaces in low-income communities remain overwhelming.

The enacting of dramatic Black masculinity while occupying public space in low-income communities creates less capacity for such men to publicly express or reconcile with the kinds of doubts, anxieties, and insecurities that come with living as Black men. A part of this experience is the denial of opportunities to live in social environments that foster healthy emotional and physical development. Indeed, the social spaces that they occupy often demand that they mask their worries and concerns, since to display them would be threatening to their social, emotional, and physical well-being. Hence, whereas it is easy to assume that Black men possess cultural orientations that direct them to the street, it is more accurate to consider that the streets are all that remain for them because they lack the material resources to avoid them or live without access to other, more private spaces for social or recreational opportunities.

The twentieth-century story of public urban space and low-income African American men, then, was one of a gradual shift over time from the streets as a place of accessibility for them amidst limitations in accessing other social spaces to a site of social and self-destruction. During that time, the streets became spaces that were no longer the province of White Americans. Rather, by the end of the twentieth century the streets were highly and particularly racialized spaces. That transformation took place as the quality of life in urban communities began to decline. Hence, the streets went from sites of crowded engagement, sociability, and some purposively placed pockets of vice activity, to sites of extreme violence, destitution, and despair. Along with that shift came a transition in public sentiment from the streets as a domain that was an always intriguing, and often exoticized, site for people with little access to private spaces to one that was inordinately hostile and insidious. The imaginations of those who felt threatened by the more contemporary reading of the streets were crystallized by the images constructed about it in the media and on television. Ultimately, this meant that distant observers could maintain a vivid picture of the streets without having to actually access them. The changing public reaction to the streets, and especially to the African American males who inhabited them, mirrored the patterns of change in the vision that sociologists held throughout the twentieth century of African American men in the urban community, and especially on the streets (Young 2016).

A conundrum confronting African American men and exacerbating their profligate public image is that while the streets became less safe throughout the latter half of the twentieth century, there has been no alternative site for them to engage in important and self-affirming activities of everyday social life that may minimize or counter the effects of vulnerability. Being on the street meant susceptibility to being observed. Those observations often take the form of surveillance by police and legal authorities, and news media and other agents of information who could document what these men were doing by way of helicopter-based surveillance. The intense street-centered focus to which Black men have been subjected leads to immediate, but often simplistic portrayals of who they are and what their lives are like. Yet access to these portraits creates for distant audiences beliefs that they know and understand these men.

Our problem with Black males, then, is rooted in an increased sense of fear and anxiety about them and the communities they inhabit (Ralph and Chance 2014; Russell-Brown 2009; Venkatesh 2000, 2006; Wacquant 2001, 2005, 2010; Wilson 1987; Young 2004). As the concept of underclass has become associated with socio-economically marginalized, urban-based people of color over the past several decades, these individuals have been subjected to extremely negative readings of their social behavior. They also have been assumed to maintain flawed and fatalistic social outlooks. Rather than coming from intimate knowledge about them, these accounts of their outlook are constituted from robust images construed about their behaviors and public identities (Young 2004). After all, the imagery of the streets in urban America is seductive. It renders portraits of these men as dangerous rather than contemplative, as hostile rather than restrained. Essentially, too much attention has been given to the street as a backdrop for observing, making interpretations, and forming judgments about the behavior of African American men, such that a richer and broader plane for analyzing them has been denied.

THREE

Getting close from afar: The unhealthy gaze upon Black males

Despite the indictments, rejection, and fear directed toward Black males, many people desire to get close to them. Just like the crisis of Black males itself, that desire has existed for at least three decades. However, this desire has nothing to do with experiencing intimate connections to these men. Nor does it have to do with developing close friendships with them. Instead, the desire to get close to these men reflects a strong societal yearning to peer into their social worlds and explore their everyday lives. It is a voyeuristic enterprise.

This curiosity has been fueled by the legacy of four decades of ethnographic research on these men, beginning at a time when research on low-income communities was deemed essential for solving social inequality (O'Connor 2001; Quadagno 1994). America's "War on Poverty," launched by President Lyndon Baines Johnson in the 1960s, provided the impetus for such research as much of its focus ultimately turned to racial inequality and the urban sphere. For many, scholars and lay people alike, this was a time to learn about how the other half – America's racialized downtrodden – actually lived.

Many of the studies discussed earlier that commenced in the 1960s, and well as some others, offered intense and elaborate research, analysis, and argument about the cultural dynamics shaping the lives of low-income African Americans. This research was produced amidst a socio-political climate that affirmed that the situation for urban-based, low-income African Americans needed intervention, and some redress was found in observational studies on street corners, neighborhoods, and communities. The prosperity and vibrancy of the American economy in the early 1960s buttressed the blossoming idea that, if understood and addressed assertively, poverty could be obliterated, or at least managed effectively in US society (Hodgson 1976; O'Connor 2001). Under the pretense that the social problems afflicting African Americans, especially those residing in disadvantaged urban communities, could be fixed once they were better understood, the 1960s-era research agenda turned to detailed considerations of people who seemed so divorced from the American Dream.

A strong and enduring premise for the research at this time was that the cultural dimensions of African American life could be thoroughly documented and then addressed. The calling of that day was to make sense of what appeared to outside observers to be extreme (but also, in some cases, rather subtle) differences in the behaviors of such people when compared against a constructed middle-class normative referent. As some of this behavior was considered fatalistic, one of the key issues of concern for researchers and the general public was how such behavior could be transformed so that urban, low-income African Americans could better attain the good life that they, and other Americans, so deeply desired. Behavior became a logical point of emphasis for these researchers as the urban American landscape became populated with underemployed and unemployed African American men whose idleness was reflected by their congregating in highly visible public spaces (i.e., parks, vacant lots, etc.) and on street corners. If such men were not visibly idle in the midst of occupying public space, they presumably were involved in gangs and illicit activity, and that was, simply enough, taken to be inappropriate behavior.

Moreover, the gaze toward Black men at that time was fueled by terms like "subculture," which were employed as scaffolding for discussion of the presumably unique and different norms, values, and attitudes demonstrated by these men. Rainwater and other social scientists argued for a consistent and robust notion of lower-class subculture (Berger 1960; Bordua 1961; Cloward and Ohlin 1960;

Cohen and Hodges 1963; Coser 1965, Gans 1962, 1969; Miller 1958; Rainwater 1970; Rodman 1963; Suttles 1968; Whyte 1943). The idea was advanced that sub-cultures were created by members of subordinate social groups contending with the difficulty of achieving the goals and desires that the larger social system considered legitimate (Abrahams 1964; Hannerz 1969; Liebow 1967; Riessman 1962; Schultz 1969). These goals and desires either were beyond the means of members of the lower echelon group, or not attainable in the ways that they were for those in more privileged positions (Rodman 1963).

This kind of vision of low-income African Americans was not very distant from that cultivated by adherents to the culture-of-poverty thesis. Anthropologist Oscar Lewis coined the term "culture of poverty" (1959, 1961, 1966). Although he said much less, and also something a little different, about the culture of poverty than has usually been attributed to him, his use of the term solidified social scientific and popular conceptions of the power of cultural forces for determining the social outcomes of those living in poverty, and his sustained portraits of the racialized poor, and Black men in particular, as culturally distinct from others.

The intense preoccupation with the public persona of low-income African American men in 1960s-era ethnography provided ample grounds for readers to conceive of such people as unlike others in mainstream America. The standard depiction, as we have seen, was that they associated on publicly visible street corners in demonstrations of bravado and swagger. As the Black Power movement came into being in the latter half of the 1960s, images of the Black Panthers marching with berets, leather jackets, and guns in hand were compounded by pictures of Black Americans rioting in response to the assassination of Martin Luther King and the perceived slowness of social change in the US. By the end of the 1960s vivid portraits of the angry Black male could be registered in any US household that had a television set.

Unlike the 1960s, when large numbers of White Americans lived in what is today known as the inner city, the 1980s notion of the underclass emerged immediately after many White Americans fled the core of many US cities (Farley et al. 2000). This meant that increasing numbers of White Americans learned about the experiences and plight of low-income Black Americans less from personal contact and observation and more from media or publicly disseminated research. Myriad images of the underclass proliferated throughout that period.

Despite the continued effort to get close to low-income African American men, a fact of modern American life is that there is extreme distance – geographic and otherwise – between them and those whose lives involve access to greater socio-economic resources and privilege. Accordingly, many of those that want to peer into the lives of these men did not desire to share in their world in any literal sense. These outsiders only wanted to know as much as they could about how these men live, and they acquired this knowledge from a very safe distance. Many in the broader American public may not personally know a socio-economically disadvantaged Black man, yet people can still articulate a great deal about their social character and their daily lives.

More troubling than the public's desire to get close to but remain physically far removed from these men is that the mechanisms of accessing them has left the broader public with a narrowly construed vision of who they are. That vision involved little to no capacity to see these men as anything but a culturally differentiated – and actually culturally flawed – segment of society. Portrayals of Black males in mainstream film did the work of vividly illustrating the very images of such men that came to mind in media and scholarly depictions of them in the age of the underclass. Tough, determined, aggressive, and dramatic Black men appeared on screens in the 1970s with the rise of Blaxploitation-era cinema. Prior to the Blaxploitation era, black actors rarely had leading roles in widely distributed films. With the arrival of the genre, they often could choose their roles, and frequently the storylines were built around their respective characters. However, these films featured black actors and were largely targeted to the African American community. During the first half of the decade, more than 200 movies of that type were produced. They broke many of the existing stereotypes of African American men in film by presenting images of Black masculinity that reflected grit and sexuality (Guerrero 2012; Koven 2010).

The males in these films often were involved in drug dealing, violence, and casual sex. The roles often included pimps street hustlers, and drug dealers. Some of the more popular films of this genre included *Super Fly* (1972), where actor Ron O'Neal portrayed a drug kingpin named Priest who was sophisticated, stylish, and popular with women, lived in plush comfort, drove the latest-model car, and wore a cocaine spoon as a fashion accessory. *Sweet Sweetback's Baadasssss Song*, which starred Melvin Van Peebles, featured a hero who was raised among prostitutes and is arrested for a crime he did not commit. During his arrest, he saves a young black male from a police beating by attacking the (White) police officers. Another film, *Shaft*, featured Richard Roundtree as detective John Shaft, who could relate to the stereotypical street corner figures found in disadvantaged urban communities, but who could also uphold and defend the law with conviction and determination. *Shaft* was made on a $500,000 budget yet grossed $13 million (or close to $70 million in today's figures), indicating how much of a public appetite there was for this new kind of film portrayal, despite the relatively low budget afforded to a film with Black protagonists. *Black Caesar* featured actor Fred Williamson, who plays a street smart hoodlum who worked his way up to being the crime boss of Harlem. Finally, *Three the Hard Way* featured actors Fred Williamson, Jim Kelly, and Jim Brown as activists working to stop a white supremacist plot to eliminate all Blacks by placing a serum in the public water supply. These and other films depicted Black men as socially influential, which was a novel turn for cinema of the era, but they were also portrayed as physically powerful and intimidating, which further cemented the public script of Black men.

By the 1980s, when the age of the underclass had come into being, the cinematic imagery continued to register toughness, determination, and aggression, but often by focusing on younger adult Black males or adolescents, all of whom seemed to be wiser than their ages would suggest given the circumstances and situations bearing upon their lives. Even if some of this work ultimately was critical or challenging of the mainstream depiction of Black males, films such as *Boyz n the Hood*, *Jason's Lyric*, *Menace II Society*, and *New Jack City* brought to the screen images of gang life, drug dealing, and social conflict that were firmly embedded in the imagery that had been crystallized by the connotations associated with the underclass.

These films were part of a more general proliferation of Hip Hop culture, which became a staple referent for Black urban life in the 1980s and beyond. Some have argued that the early years of Blaxploitation films profoundly impacted contemporary Hip Hop culture as several prominent artists, such as Snoop Dogg, Big Daddy Kane, and Ice-T, adopted various personas exemplifying the kind of character made prominent in those films. The emergence of gangster rap in the 1990s exacerbated the imagery of aggression, hostility, social threat, and extreme indulgence that had been codified in the rise of the underclass.

Film makers such as Spike Lee (in *Do the Right Thing*) and John Singleton (in *Boyz n the Hood*) strove to problematize the narrow image of Black masculinity that was promoted in many of the other films produced at the time of their efforts. However, their contributions did not disrupt the overall pattern of introducing a particular image of Black masculinity and Black men into the gaze of a public that otherwise did not have to invest in intimate nor long-term associations with the very people to which this imagery was connected.

The legacy of such portraits of Black men and black masculinity did more than create a consumable image for majority America. It also presented Black males with a public image and identity of Black masculinity that they had to contend with even if they did not endorse it. That black males often believe that they must exemplify or validate various kinds of vulgar or rugged masculinities that have been associated with them, even if they do not personally adhere to these depictions, has been well documented in social-science research (Ford 2008, 2011; Hunter and Davis 1992). In some cases, their doing so often appears to them as a prerequisite for attaining the social and physical security necessary to engage everyday life in turbulent communities (Anderson 1990; Ford 2011; Majors and Billson 1992). This very imagery also came to surface in highly problematic ways in intimate relations (Neal 2006, 2013).

* * * * *

The research and policy creation that took place during the middle of the twentieth century opened the door onto Black life for much of white America. Despite very noble and deliberate efforts to correct the malaise of the social condition for African Americans at that time, a consequence of directing attention to that constituency was an intrigue, if not infatuation, with the

African American urban scenario. A primary point of attention in looking at that scenario, whether through civic initiative, media, or cinema, was the Black male. What ultimately became an iconic image of Black males came into being and was proliferated.

The principal effect of this proliferation was misunderstanding, even as mainstream America was strongly invited to absorb an image of Black males. What was ignored during this transmission of images was the extent to which Black men embrace a rich multiplicity of roles in their communities that transcend the highly stigmatized imagery associated with them. They are brothers, fathers, sons, neighbors. Yet the image of them that is crystallized denies them any public identity that does not reference their being a social problem. Consequently, they are viewed through a highly judgmental lens, often derived from a narrow focus on their behavior as the only dimension of their humanity made available to outside observers.

There is more to the culture of low-income African American men than four decades of public attention has brought forth. The flawed public depiction of Black males is a consequence of the extreme preoccupation in the US with their behavior and lifestyles rather than with their interpretations and analyses. The limited knowledge circulated to mainstream America about them too easily leads to a general public sentiment of despair and hopelessness for those most sensitive to their plight. For those less compassionate, the promotion of rugged black masculinity and all that is associated with it leads to anxiety, anger, and rebuff. Whatever the case may be, each type of response blinds the public to envisioning Black males in alternative, and much healthier and appropriate, ways.

Black males have been subjected to extremely negative readings of their social behavior and their dispositions. They also have been assumed to maintain flawed and fatalistic social outlooks. Often, these accounts are presumptions rather than directly informed understandings because the external parties that make them do not necessarily have access to the inner feeling and beliefs of Black males. Rather than coming from intimate knowledge about them, these accounts of their outlook are constituted from the images construed from their behaviors and public identities (Young 2004). The challenge, however, is to look both at and beyond their behavior. Investing in more thorough understandings of how African American men think and feel is a necessary corrective to academic and public attention to how they appear and act in public. Indeed, the very claim that these males have feelings – sometimes in regard to their relationships to criminal activity, violence, and the possibilities of death or substantive bodily harm, but also to family, peers, and community more generally – and that these feelings carry an intensity and complication not fully revealed by their public actions, and that they think about their social realities more provocatively than may be realized when focusing only on their actions, necessarily invites a bold rethinking of them.

FOUR

Pushing past pathology: Undoing the consequences of the negative gaze

Moving beyond pathological framing that circumscribes Black men involves a deliberate mental effort. It means being prepared to see more of Black men than is immediately apparent. An important step toward doing so is attending to how some of these men argue for and attempt to reconstruct their own public identities and, as we shall see later in this chapter, by how they strive to serve other Black men who prototypically appear to be in crisis. Whatever their approach happens to be, their struggle is immense.

The first type of effort, the reconstructing of one's own identity, was conveyed to me during my service as a consultant for the Transitional Jobs Reentry Demonstration Project. The project, administered by the Manpower Demonstration Research Corporation, involved an analysis of the re-entry experiences of male participants in a transitional jobs initiative. Aside from receiving the temporary subsidized jobs, the men received support services, and formal job placement assistance (Redcross et al. 2010). My role in the evaluation of the four-city project was to periodically interview and shadow 10 men in each of the project's focal cities (Detroit, Chicago, Milwaukee, and St. Paul).

Felon, just the word, period, frightens people because they don't really know. Some people don't give you a chance because of the word "felon." ("Basil")

I did my crime so long ago and I served my time, but I still have the "X" on my back...I ain't hurt nobody or kill nobody, so it shouldn't be held against me for life for something that I was doing when I was young. ("Terrance")

People don't see me as just an ex-offender anymore; I am their coworker, or the guy that's good at driving or greeting the customers. [Being a former inmate] means that I'm not doing the things that I used to do. I'm bettering myself. A life of crime wasn't for me. It's not for me now, but back then when I was offending, I didn't care about it. I just wanted to commit crimes. Now, I know because I'm better out here than in there [prison], and everybody needs me out here. I'm useless in there...My family, when things go wrong or support or something, whenever they need something, they need me here, or even just to talk to them, or even just family gatherings, they'd rather see me there than coming up to see me [in prison] ... [People] respect me for what I'm doing and how I was able to make that change. ("Chris")

I met Basil, Terrance, and Chris in 2008 while working on the Demonstration Project. In looking back on my three years of fieldwork there, this was my first research opportunity to focus exclusively on the kinds of Black men that seemingly were most doomed in the US. The crimes that the Black men that I encountered in this project were convicted of included homicide, burglary, assault, and narcotics distribution. Accordingly, some of them typified the most ominous kinds of Black men that others could imagine. Yet, my work in this project necessarily required an effort to look beyond their pasts and to consider how they contended with the possibility of a better future. This effort included having the chance to witness their efforts to act outside of the boundaries of the imagery often associated with the criminal element, especially Black male criminals.

Basil, Terrance, and Chris were former drug dealers who also spent much of their adolescence and young adulthood engaged in a wide variety of other illegal activities. Basil and Terrance were not successful in finding full-time work during my involvement with them for the assessment. That being the case, their comments reflect the kind of despair and frustration that comes with the absence of such an opportunity. More importantly, these remarks recall the ease with which Black men can be pegged as unworthy people and the deep emotional impact that such treatment can have. When put on paper, it is difficult to pierce through their comments to understand that the pain and suffering they were experiencing results from such stigmatization. Of course, some may feel that these men deserve to be so stigmatized. Yet, the problem at hand is not only one of whether these men deserve an opportunity to move beyond their pasts (after all, they did serve their sentences after being sanctioned for their transgressions). The problem is also a matter of what it means for Black men to bear the consequences of being perceived as criminally inclined, or unworthy of the kinds of self-improvement opportunities that most people would seek.

Sociologist Devah Pager has studied extensively how Black men, irrespective of their particular pasts, are assumed to be actual or potential criminals by employers who encountered them in interview settings (Pager 2007). Through a series of audit studies, she uncovered the extent to which merely appearing at an interview allowed Black men to be regarded by the interviewer as an actual or potential criminal, even if the constructed resume for those individuals was of equal quality to the

White American men who were included in her audit studies of how potential employers react to Black men. The story of Theodore (a pseudonym), also a participant in the re-entry project, makes the case as well:

> The biggest crock that they can give you in the world is that a man can be convicted in these courts, and then serve his time and he's paid his debt... Though I made those decisions to do those crimes and got myself in those situations, I'm still paying another debt each time they say no or each time they turn me away... It kind of fulfills the dream that people make us out to be and that's why they turn us away... I'm five years from 50. I'm getting scared, like, how long can I keep struggling? I'm getting up there.

In contrast to the other men, Chris represents an alternative story. Soon after being released from a Wisconsin penitentiary, he was fortunate enough to get placed in a transition job in a supermarket. Accordingly, he has spent his post-incarceration time working as a delivery man and stock person. Aside from his remarks that appear at the start of this chapter, he told me that having a job meant that not only did he become a new man to himself, but others learned to accept him as someone different than who he used to be. That latter transformation is crucial for the quest of ensuring Black men are not doomed. Chris' account of public identity transformation is the extreme version of the kind of transformation that must be afforded to Black men more generally in society. The first step in undoing the consequences of the long-standing gaze upon Black males is the very demystification of the negative image cast upon them.

Implicit in Chris' story is that he found himself successfully immersed into the social world of people other than Black Americans. Even though that immersion was only by way of working in a high-end supermarket that catered to more privileged people (it was one with a delivery service), it created a platform by which those others could see him differently. His employers knew of his background (because his ability to garner that employment was based upon his being an ex-offender), so they experienced first-hand the transition of his public identity from negative to positive. Such transformation is not easy, nor does it unfold in the same way for every Black male fortunate enough to engage it. Hence, the critical work to be done begins with those who stand apart from Black men preparing themselves to re-think them. This means developing a mindset about Black men that allows for redemption rather than for permanent indictment. It also means opening up consideration of their behavior as not always reactive or focused on the destructive, but rather as produced out of fear or uncertainty as much as (and sometimes more so than) deliberation.

* * * * *

The hard work required to reconstitute the image of Black men is revealed in the efforts of two older Black men that I encountered while doing research in Chicago. These men were, to use the vernacular that they employed about themselves, "old heads." The concept of the old head has been written about by sociologist Elijah Anderson, who describes old heads as fathers, uncles, grandfathers, or neighbors, figures who serve as models of success in past years, and who can often provide wisdom and counsel for younger generations of men and women (Anderson 1999).

In his own work Elijah Anderson has been concerned that old heads were not paid much attention by the younger generation, who are caught up in more immediate gratification and campaigns for respect. This respect was not garnered in the same way when the old heads were young. Instead, at that time they went to work in the industrial sphere and earned respect by bringing home a salary and providing for their families. Anderson makes the point that such work tends not to be available nowadays, nor do the interests of the younger generation allow them to heed the kinds of advice given by many old heads.

The two men I introduce here are not quite the kinds of old heads that Anderson talks about. In fact, each of them was much more like the troubled youth that Anderson says now avoid the advice of the older generation. I have told much about their story before (Young 2007), but say some other things here in order to build a case about what is at stake in thinking anew about Black men. The first "old head," Smittie (a pseudonym), was in his mid-forties when I first met him in the mid-1990s. He was born in New York City but raised in Chicago. As a young child he moved with his family into the Henry Horner Homes on Chicago's Near West Side. Smittie's father was killed by one of his former wives (not Smittie's mother). Smittie grew up with mom and stepdad and had eight siblings in the family. The conditions of a crowded household were compounded by his stepfather's physical abuse of his mother, which Smittie said persisted throughout his childhood.

Since his adolescence in the 1960s, Smittie has been a gang member in a faction of the Vice Lord Nation, an associate of the Chicago chapter of the Black Panther Party and a participant in some of their community organizing efforts, a full-time employee for nearly a decade in domestic service at the Playboy Club of Chicago, and since the mid-1980s chronically unemployed.

Milton (also a pseudonym) is close in age to Smittie. He never knew his father, and throughout his life his mother worked as a domestic or in retail services. He has eight brothers and sisters. Other than Milton, only one sibling has completed college. The rest have work histories ranging from steady blue-collar employment to chronic unemployment.

Milton grew up in various South Side Chicago neighborhoods until his teenage years when the family settled in the working-class community of Englewood. Although he reported being a solid student academically, Milton was better known as a standout high-school athlete in the early 1960s. He played both basketball and American football and was actively recruited by various major American college programs in both sports (he informed me that his basketball skills were far superior, and these drew the majority of the recruiters' attention). However, unlike more recent times when professional sport careers are contemplated by talented high-school athletes, Milton knew of very few people who ever made it to the professional ranks from his background in the 1960s. Hence, he determined to embark upon his quest for a new and exciting experience away from the blight of Chicago that did not include preparing for sports.

Rather than attend college, confusion and curiosity about the world led Milton to leave high school before graduating and enter the military. He believed that this would allow him to explore his curiosity at the expense of the federal government. Milton enlisted in the US Marine Corps and planned to earn his GED (general equivalency diploma) there. Instead, he soon found himself in combat in Vietnam.

While in Vietnam, Milton began ingesting narcotics, beginning with marijuana, which over the next few years led to an addiction to heroin. From the late 1960s until the early 1980s he sold drugs, stolen goods, and involved himself in various kinds of underground economic activity. Milton told me that he figured that he made close to half a million dollars selling narcotics. As he was an addict throughout that time, he was in no shape to save any of it. Instead, by 1980 Milton had a criminal record and had experienced a revolving-door pattern of short-term incarcerations. By the late 1980s he determined that he would have to change his life or he would face death on the streets of California, where he was then living. Choosing the former, he borrowed the car of a drug supplier and drove himself to a rehabilitation clinic. Since that time, things turned quite positive for him. He successfully completed rehabilitation and then completed his studies for his GED. Within several years he enrolled and completed studies in a California community college. Thereafter, he enrolled and received a degree from a four-year higher educational institution. He then completed some graduate study, and in the 1990s he entered into the ministry.

While starting out in similar states of constraint, Smittie and Milton experienced very different life paths. As youth and young men, both struggled in dealing with circumstances that threatened their already precarious chances to get ahead, including getting into trouble with the law. Smittie never really overcame instability and turbulence, but Milton did. Aside from their early years, where the two men also stand on similar ground is in their efforts to deal with the younger Black males in their lives. What they say about that topic informs greatly about the prospects of changing societal images of Black males.

Smittie has four nephews. When I met him he was living with his mother and one of them. He is now an "old gangster," too old to be heavily involved in gang activity, but familiar enough to the young breed that were active at the time when we spoke. He told me, "I have three generations of gang fighters, gang members in my family now. And I spawned that... I'm so embarrassed by it though, I mean the kind of problems that they could bring to the family, you know, the grief and shit. I mean, that's a terrible sight – seeing one of your people laying up there with a hole in his head or back, or cold dead."

The contradiction that he has lived and that he now sees in his nephews about being in a gang ruptures any sense that these men can be thought of as simply good or bad. Their life circumstances left them with limited choices. They were involved in the gang life for survival, but as Smittie knew full well, risked survival as a result of their immersion within it. As he said:

> They have to protect themselves in the community, you know. It's basically a protection thing. People will try to intimidate you. They will take from you. They will abuse you physically. So you know, if you live through it, then you have accomplished a lot. You survived it. But a lot of times they don't. They don't live through it, you know, because of the mentality of a lot of our youths today.

Smittie's comments need to be taken in the context of his own past experiences as a gang member. As he saw it, the mere existence of gangs was not the problem. Smittie was an elder and a respected figure in that world. I witnessed this by how much deference he received from younger men in the community as I conducted fieldwork with them. His concern for the younger men was about the absence of formal opportunities for employment and thus the availability of more free time for frivolous gang activities that could bring harm or sanction to gang members. In Smittie's mind this was the root cause of the wanton violence that he believes that modern gangs promote. He told me that increasing the opportunities for these young men would allow them not to have to be so deeply embedded in neighborhood gangs and the exacerbating aggression and violence that came with it. As he said:

> There's some guys so crazy now with the different organizations out here. They just kill each other just for any, I mean anything. Just name it and they'll do it....And a lot of these young brothers don't have the opportunities to grow because they're so caught up with that peer pressure. And they'll never grow out of it because like I say once you get trapped into the organizations, it's just a matter of time before you're either dead, or you kill somebody or somebody kills you. You know, I mean it's just that obvious.

Smittie and many men like him have a vision of what is going on and what needs to be done for Black men in crisis. Yet, men like him are often not recognized as such. Including the perspective of men like Smittie in the public conversation validates their identity as something other than men in trouble, but men who are sensitive, aware, and, if given opportunities, agents who can respond to the conditions and circumstances in their lives.

Those with no connection whatsoever to communities like the one where Smittie lives may see the answer in the mere elimination of gangs as the solution to the problem. Clearly, as Smittie saw it, the legacy of their existence dismisses any notion that they can simply be made to disappear. The realities of his and other Black males' lives in Chicago meant that for him, gangs were a critical resource in an otherwise resource-depleted environment. They provided protection as much as they facilitated danger and, as they saturated the social world of low-income Chicago, Black men who resided there had to be content with them. For Smittie, then, the flawed logic of avoidance was replaced by an emphasis on cautious action and forethought as the best mechanisms for survival. Smittie elaborates on his perspective by telling the following story:

So one night about ten-thirty I was waiting on the Madison Street bus. I always have a seven-inch knife in my pocket, for these particular situations. A group of young kids came by ranging from the age of about 10 to about 15, but it was about seven or eight of 'em, right? And one of them asked me, "What was I riding?" – meaning what gang was I in. I told him, "The Madison bus to work, to take care of my family." I told him, "The Madison bus." He said, "You are a smart M-F, you know?" And I said, "Look brother, please, get you some business. I'm on my way to work." One of them picked up a 40-ounce beer bottle and hit me in my head with it. Now, by that time I done pulled my knife out and I grabbed him. He was ten years old. And I threw this kid on the ground and I was fitting to stab him. And I looked at him, and I said, "It would be a waste of my life if I hit this kid in his head with this knife." And he was, "Please mister, don't kill me. Please don't kill me." And meanwhile his buddies had ran off and found sticks and stuff. And I actually ran from these kids so I wouldn't hurt them, or I wouldn't get hurt.

Smittie obviously had no reservations about possibly getting violent with these youths. As a young man who once stood in their position, he was quite familiar with the kind of situation that he faced and how he had to respond to it. He knew he was faced with a group of youth who were looking for trouble. Yet, his willingness to handle the situation in the manner that he did also demonstrated that he was very much a part of their social world and cognizant of how to best operate in it.

In telling his story, Smittie reflects much of what distant observers might consider to be a part of the problem with Black males. He was unwilling to back down. He was aggressive. Most importantly, he was prepared to respond to counter violence with violence. He clearly did not exhibit weakness nor timidity. What he also expressed in telling his story, however, was that he was not uncritically prone to violence. This old head and former gang member knew full well what he was doing to protect and defend himself at the particular point in time that he did it, and he knew what it would mean in a larger context if he had to fully act out on what appeared to be his initial intentions. Part of the damnation of Black males rests in their being regarded as uncritically violent. However, Smittie was far from uncritical that evening. He was both conscious of the scenario he found himself in and conscientious about how he would manage it. It is that blend of response that would have been lost if Smittie was forced to act on his initial impulse, and criminal charges were to have come his way. If the latter were the case, he would have been pegged as another dangerous Black man acting irresponsibly to do harm to others and possibly himself.

Another one of his stories also makes this case for how insight into his conscientiousness adds more depth to his character. Here Smittie tells about the tribulations of trying to support and guide one of his nephews. His general approach to the four of them, as he put it in a grandfatherly tone, was to keep them from being "stuck on stupid and looking for dumb." In trying to help one nephew in particular think about the potential bad choice he was preparing to make concerning a personal conflict, Smittie said:

I had to actually drive him down on the ground physically. He had a gun. He was gonna shoot somebody over ten dollars. This was Sunday, yesterday. And I'm trying to tell him, you know, you're reacting, you're not thinking. You know, and I took the gun, you know. He actually buckled up at me. He wanted to fight, and I'm looking at him and I'm saying I see myself in him, you know. He's reacting and not thinking, you know. Over ten dollars. So what did I do? I took the gun from him. Gave him ten dollars and kicked him out. Told him I don't want to talk to him anymore. And then he came back, later on about nine or ten o'clock, "I'm sorry, I won't do that no more." I told him, "You know, you don't react. You think first. There's a lot of goddamn humps in the ground out there in Burr Oak (cemetery) from people reacting and not thinking." You know, I try to express that to him. You know, because I can't stop them. I can't. I mean, they've grown. I can only tell them what not to do. I'm saying, I don't want to see them in these positions (of getting into unnecessary trouble), but if they got to be there, if you gotta be there, you gotta be smart. You can't be stuck on stupid looking for dumb. Straight up you have to be smart. That's as simple as that.

Smittie told me that he was the only male relative in the lives of his nephews. As such he was about much more than trying to correct their behavior. More importantly, he suspended making moral judgments in favor of trying to provide practical guidance. The latter, he well knew, was what could keep them alive. In striving to do that, he was pursuing, in his own particular way, a moral project. It also was all that he could do given that he, himself, survived life as a gang member, possessed a rich and broad repertoire of street wisdom, and was keenly aware of the kinds of mistakes young Black men can make and, therefore, how they might be avoided.

Milton also told me that there were not many men around in his family to talk to the younger males. His filling that vacancy meant that he could marshal his past, as a former athlete, war veteran, substance abuser, and hustler, to provide guidance to the young men in his family. Milton told me that his stature in his family was heightened by his having overcome an addiction. He was, in the eyes of his relatives, a survivor. His example, therefore, was especially meaningful when interacting with the family.

Milton has more than two dozen nieces and nephews. Although he does not reside with any of them, he said that he is the point person for advice and counsel in the extended family. His presence was especially critical for the children of his siblings who have experienced substance-abuse problems as well as extreme economic hardship. He told me that he had been asked into situations that involved drugs, gangs, and the police. In one case in particular Milton talked about a nephew who is following his own early life pattern of drug abuse and distribution. Milton informed me that he caused part of this nephew's problem because he introduced him into narcotics during his own years of involvement with them. Milton said that although this nephew is aware that Milton is no longer involved in that kind of activity, he holds no illusions about being able to singlehandedly transform his nephew. As he explained:

You know, because basically what he's going through now is the same road I went through, you know, in terms of being out there in those streets, you know, on your own, and basically just looking to get high.... You know, it's like when, uh, people ask me to talk to him, I says, "Well, what am I going to tell him?" You know, he knows. I think somehow, you know, we tend to think people who are in trouble like, you know, don't know and it's something that he could tell you more about.... The last long conversation I had with him, you know, I was really shaking my head. I mean he could tell me more (than I could tell him) about the consequences, the problems, what he needs to do with his life, but right now he's just making choices.

Milton's understanding of what he believes he can and cannot do on behalf of this nephew is made clear by what more he had to say:

I mean, he just can't wake up tomorrow and say I'm not gonna do this anymore. I mean, there has to be a process. But I mean right now, he's choosing not to... I can only show him model behavior. Just, you know, let him see it. And hopefully, again, it'll just give him information that'll help him make a better decision one day. You know, maybe, maybe not.

Milton was not particularly concerned about the difficulties in trying to produce change in the young people in his life. In talking about how he approached them he said:

I share my experiences with them. And I guess my thing about kids, young people, is that, you know, the most we can do as adults is just sort of give them the information and let them know what's going on. Whether it's by way of telling them about our lives...well, I guess that's the only way to do it...so that they at some point will have a stash of options, you know, and they can at least know, you know, what they're choosing when they do become smart enough to make choices, you know, and stuff. I don't preach any particular philosophy to them, but I do model on things....I just try to, you know, model that as a way hoping that they will see that....Or at some point if they don't go that way, but they're caught in a situation where they can reach out and make a choice then they'll know what they're choosing.

Milton said that it is impossible to predetermine the outcomes of his efforts. As he put it:

You know, it's difficult to know. I would assume that it's just they take out things and just store it, you know, it just becomes part of other information that they get, you know, and at some point they dissect it themselves and figure out how to use it, you know.

The root causes of the current social problems in the community of African American youth was not lost on Smittie or Milton. As Smittie put it:

Money. Drugs. Uh, drugs. Definitely drugs has a lot to do with it. Just like any other enterprise or business, you want to expand it. And when you expand it you're going to run into peaks and valleys, and how do you solve that? You either climb it or go under it. And a lot of times they just go through it.... Not only with the drugs, but I mean a 14-year-old walk up to a, drive up to a burly 40-year-old man and shoot him in the back of the head [which occurred to a friend and fellow gang member of Smittie's several weeks before our conversation]? C'mon, that's ridiculous.

Both Milton and Smittie understood without ambiguity that having a presence in their nephews' lives did not mean they were able to easily direct or influence them. Although each had much to say about how they tried to intervene in the lives of younger relatives, each also knew their limitations. Their own experiences best informed each of them about what they could expect from the young men that they tried to counsel. Their sense of limitation was a by-product of their intimate connection to and involvement in similar circumstances concerning troubled youth. More importantly, though, their accounts each encourage very different thinking about Black men who are or have been immersed into crises.

Milton's last comment in particular highlights how well each understood and connected to the young men in their lives. Each saw something more than troubled young men, even if such men often were in, or on the verge of being in, huge trouble. Each did not indict nor explicitly chastise the young men in their lives, or at least did not make such efforts the sole means by which they related to them. In short, each strove to connect with the humanity of these young men in ways that did not dismiss, but included more than, the narrow portrait of them as debauched or degenerate.

There are lessons to be learned from how they represent themselves as well as how they engage the young men in their lives. In the case of the former, Smittie and Milton believe themselves to be survivors. They are products of the kind of low-income, urban, African American communities whose residents sometimes engaged in the reckless and often self-destructive behaviors that are often associated with such places. In contending with these conditions, Milton argued quite forcefully that he made his own choices in life, including the choice to pursue the military while not yet finished with high school and to commit to ingesting narcotics over a nearly 20-year period. That mentality, together with his having survived near-death encounters in Vietnam and living for nearly two decades with his substance-abuse problem, equipped him with a wide range of experiences to think about and apply in interacting with his nieces and nephews. It also allowed him the capacity to regard himself as highly efficacious. After all, he had overcome all the negativity that he had experienced. He felt that he eventually chose to do so as much as he chose to begin ingesting drugs. Similarly, while not having overcome poverty, Smittie also saw himself as efficacious because he was a senior-level gang member who reached an age that many of his childhood associates had not, and Smittie had done so while continuing to reside in the same impoverished community where he had been born and had engaged risk and peril as a younger man.

Smittie and Milton demonstrate that being older and beyond the fast life did not have to mean a complete loss of status in that domain. Both of these men were listened to and respected by the younger people in their lives. This was due to the fact that, in the course of engaging younger people, Smittie and Milton were decidedly less judgmental than would be many casual observers of the individuals for whom they provided counsel. Neither Smittie nor Milton remained fixed on the immorality of illegal or violent activity that their relatives were immersed in, but, instead, saw those pursuits as understandable options for troubled people to pursue in deprived communities. They also saw these people, their relatives, as committed to making their behavioral choices according to their own standards and measures. The goal, as Smittie aptly put it, was simply to help them keep from being stuck on stupid, and looking for dumb.

What Smittie and Milton deliver is something other than a call for the kind of morally grounded response from younger people that is more traditionally taken to be the proper contribution of old heads (Anderson 1999). Instead, they call for the recognition that such young people ultimately will make their own choices and that while the intervention of the old head can mitigate in the presence of certain crises (as Smittie tried to do when his nephew planned to shoot someone), he cannot change the dispositions of people who do not want to change.

In arguing about the traditional old head, Anderson (1999: 71) said that such a figure's functioning centered on the transmission of values concerning hard work and other explicit characteristics. Anderson also argued that today such old heads have lost most of their esteemed social status (pp. 72, 272). However, what is gained by paying attention to these two old heads, aside from the fact that they are not of the type that Anderson had in mind in his writings, is both a deeper and more complex rendering of Black males. On the one hand, they reflect a combination of traits denied to these men when seen only as constituent parts of a great American social problem. On the other, they reflect a manner of engaging men in trouble that allows for imagining new possibilities and approaches to push past simply patholo-gizing Black males. Instead, their efforts invite imposing a new lens on such men – one that recognizes that they can be reflective and make choices, and that they may know more about who they are and what they choose to do then others allow them to know (even if they are not always positioned to effectively correct themselves).

FIVE

Conclusions: The promise of looking anew at Black males

Several years ago I was invited to deliver a lecture at a predominantly African American Baptist church in a small city in southeastern Michigan. This lecture was a part of a special event organized by the church leadership to address the plight of Black men in the US. Since the mid-1990s it was not uncommon for many Baptist and other African American community-serving churches to host what they called "lock-ins" to examine the situation of these males. The lock-ins consisted of the male members of the church and invited guests coming together for a full evening of conversation and fellowship. Those gathered for the event would spend the night in the church in order to bond over intense and lengthy discussion about the plight of Black men and the possibilities for improving their situation. Implicit in many of these gatherings was an emphasis on what the men needed to do for one another in regard to that agenda. Thus, personal responsibility, a staple of Black

77

church discourse, was an integral point of attention in these gatherings.

The event that I attended was not an overnight lock-in. Rather, this one involved a few hours of conversation, beginning with two presentations (including my own) and a dinner. My presentation was the second of that evening. It followed one given by a former professional football player. He talked about making the competitive nature of Black men a more positive factor in family and community settings (throughout his talk he also directed us through a lot of chanting and clapping). My presentation involved sharing some statistics and information about the state of Black men in the US, as well as in the very community where the church was located. I also shared my thoughts about what needed to be done to address the so-called crisis of Black males. I spoke about what Black men must do to take better care of themselves: socially, emotionally, and physically. I also spoke about what needed to be done in US society at large so that Black men could be viewed more appropriately, and potentially more favorably, by other US citizens.

The presentation was followed by an open conversation by the several dozen men in attendance at the church. They shared their hopes and dreams for the future. They also raised their concerns and questions about the present situation and circumstances for Black men. In the middle of the conversation one of the assistant pastors of the church took the floor and declared that he had been deliberately hiding a part of his past from the congregation and the church leadership. He said that he was an ex-convict. He explained that for a period of his adult life he had served time in a state penitentiary. The rest of the men in the room immediately fell silent. He said that he had never shared this part of his past with anyone in the church, especially as he determined to enter into the ministry sometime after his release, and wanted to pursue life as a man of God without others having insight into his profligate past. It was important to him, he said, to cultivate an identity as someone prepared to serve the Lord and not someone who once upon a time did things terrible enough to merit a prison sentence.

We were gathered in the basement of a church that was not particularly distinguishable from the kind found in working-class African American communities. It was very nondescript, and the church itself was slightly smaller than the parking lot surrounding it. It faced a row of public housing units located immediately west of it. Hence, I gathered that the head pastor did not necessarily engage the kind of vetting process in hiring his team that might be expected in a larger and more elaborate church. Therefore, I was not surprised that an assistant pastor could show up with this kind of background and not be found out. However, I was captivated by the very moment that was unfolding. That night the assistant pastor said that he felt compelled to tell those of us gathered in that basement that he was an ex-offender because that evening of sharing encouraged him to feel that he could now share with us this very private part of himself.

The effect of his disclosure was powerful and penetrating. It was clear to me that many of the men of the gathering, who had known this pastor for some time, and certainly much longer than I had, having only met him for the first time that evening, were surprised to learn about his history. More importantly, though, they were fully prepared to accept and embrace him given what he reported to us that evening. When he finished speaking he received hugs and handshakes. He also received words of encouragement and tribute for courageously sharing what he did with us. I felt a sense of gratitude for being able to witness all of this. In fact, I remember this part of the evening better than anything else that took place, or even more than the details of what I said in the course of that evening.

What occurred that night was the very act of acceptance that I hope that more Black men can receive if they courageously share who they are or who they have been with the world. As evident by his behavior throughout that evening, this pastor was a mild and courteous man. Yet, by his own account, he had been a totally different kind of person several years before that evening. Going forward he wanted to be the man who he was that evening, but also a man who could be acknowledged as having the kind of past that he had been carrying inside of his head and heart for several years. I have no way of knowing what became of him in the weeks, months, and years following my visit to the church. Nor do I know how the men (and women) of that church continued to feel about him. This vacancy of knowledge does not dismiss that what he did that evening and how he was received by others created a moment that I hope could become a reality for other Black men.

* * * * *

Until he revealed his past, the assistant pastor who spoke in that small Michigan church was living a new life. He was fortunate in that he was able to create that new life himself rather than having to rely on others to accept him as a changed man. What is unfortunate for many other Black men who have had troubled pasts is that they lack the capacity to *freely* recreate themselves. Instead, their quest requires that others somehow commit to determining to see them anew.

The ability to see Black males anew is the crucial first step in eradicating the doom. There exist models for how this can be done, and some of them remain in contemporary cinema, this despite the centrality of cinema in fostering some of the problematic imagery associated with Black males. In 2017, the Academy of Motion Pictures awarded the Oscar for Best Picture to *Moonlight*. The film, directed by Barry Jenkins, was based on a play entitled, *In Moonlight Black Boys Look Blue* (written by Tarell Alvin McCraney). *Moonlight* tells the story of a Black man named Chiron, focusing on three periods in his life: early childhood, adolescence, and adulthood. Chiron first appears as a shy and withdrawn child who is fearful of bullies. He is befriended by a drug dealer (played by 2017 Academy Best Supporting Actor award winner Mahershala Ali), who demonstrates a warmth and compassion to him that is not associated with the hard and rugged lifestyle of such men. That drug dealer, Juan, becomes a father figure and a huge source of support for the frail and confused little boy. Chiron is also friends with another Black boy, Kevin, with whom he engages in a sexual act when both boys are teenagers. As an adolescent, Chiron struggles with his sexuality, his mother's drug addiction, her commitment to prostitution, and her negligence of him throughout the film. Ultimately, Chiron gets arrested for violently attacking one of his bullies, and he next appears in the film as an adult male, with considerable and solid girth, who has also become a drug dealer.

The complex character portraits in this film are only minimally conveyed through this summary. Indeed, that complexity is best revealed through viewing the film itself. What *Moonlight* delivers is the complexity of Black male characters that seems to be denied the very real Black male bodies that live their lives in the US. Among other accomplishments, *Moonlight* effectively conveys Black male hetero- and homosexuality, aggression and passivity, and anger and fear, all of which are contained in different ways within each of the two Black male bodies (Juan and Chiron). The remarkable statement that this film makes is that Black men, who are on the surface troubled, threatening, violent, and angry, can be loving, sensitive, insecure, and vulnerable. In many ways, *Moonlight* makes the point of the very pages of this book.

Of course, the reason why the public can become so immersed in film is because the images are necessarily distant from the reality. Cinema provides us with the opportunity to encounter characters, circumstances, and events without having to immediately and intimately experience them: we don't have to risk close encounters with the characters. What we must do in moving beyond the damnation of Black men, however, is to prepare ourselves to more fully and directly encounter these individuals. We must more fully and immediately include Black men into our communities, our civil society, and into our vision of humanity and of the human condition in the US.

A new vision of Black men is in order. Ultimately, what is required is a vision of Black men as vulnerable rather than only threatening. That vision is one that must be cultivated and embraced by those outside of the category of Black men. It is one that does not have to deny that which is unpleasant, objectionable, or discouraging about the kinds of activities and involvements that have constituted the lives of many Black men. However, that vision must be comprehensive of these men's inner thoughts, feelings, and interpretations about themselves and their conceptions of their place in their social worlds. It must be a more complete vision of their humanity, which includes more than what they have done or failed to do, but how they think about these aspects of their lives and how they regard the efforts and failures of their past and present lives. This vision need not rest on excuses and vindications, but rather on a more wholesome perspective that includes the behaviors and thoughts of these men that are ignored or else rendered as superficial or irrelevant when the current vision of them is as less than fully capable of engaging the modern world.

Reshaping the public image of Black men involves recasting the gaze upon them. It involves moving away from the kinds of social-problems logic that have driven the last 30 years of their public imagery and allowing a broader, deeper, and more complex portrait of Black masculinity to surface. A large part of doing so means engaging a broad conversation about the constitution of healthy contemporary African American masculinity. Much has been said in scholarship about what such masculinity should consist of and reflect (Collins 2005; Hunter and Davis 1992). In this work an explosion of new portraits and images has emerged that has created space for men who are quite distant from the traditional depictions of Black masculinity. Included here are gay, bisexual, and transgender men, and those who do not embrace aggression or popular notions of toughness. The mandate asserted by these scholars and others is to invite these men into normalcy.

Also included is a challenge to the notion that healthy masculinity requires the status of head of household rather than partner in the management of the household. It means that Black boys are to be regarded as children, and not men in children's bodies. Therefore, the still problematic feelings of threat extended to adult men should not be brought to bear upon young males who have yet to live life as adults. It also means the freedom to express and address vulnerability in its various forms, whether associated with social relations, sexuality, health, physical and mental ability, or otherwise. The new imagination of Black males should encourage re-thinking of these men as not simply troubled or potentially troubling individuals who are eternally configured as needing to make societal amends, but as individuals who must be given the opportunity to learn how to effectively contribute to and draw from their families and communities in order to become healthy, proactive, and productive individuals.

Public awareness and comprehension of the situation of African American men must be re-oriented such that the range of issues and concerns pertaining to this constituency (e.g., fatherhood, employment, educational attainment, incarceration, and physical health and well-being) is considered in an integrated and mutually reinforcing way. Shifting the public conversation in media, policy, and other arenas must be done in ways that do not allow for a collapsing back into simplistic indictments of these men as adherents to flawed or profligate value systems and normative orders. Instead, and as evidenced by Smittie, Milton, and some of the other men introduced in the preceding pages, the objective must be to better document and advance understandings of how choice-making is situated in cultural systems of meaning-making that are not inherently degenerate. What must be acknowledged, accepted, and validated are visions of Black men as vulnerable beings that require safe spaces for coming to terms with their vulnerabilities in healthy ways.

One step toward achieving this end is that researchers and others must commit to the idea that the street must be rethought as a site for the cultural expression of Black masculinity. The critical challenge at hand, then, is first to more seriously separate out as analytically distinct how these men engage the street in terms of their behavior, and how they mentally and emotionally engage it. When more attention is given to that latter domain of engagement, a different, broader, more penetrating, and more essential plane for the cultural analysis of these men comes into being. It provides a space for others to consider that many of these men are reflective about different aspects of their lives, unsure and uncertain about some of what they have to confront and experience in their lives, and critically questioning about some aspects in ways that their prior behavior alone could not possibly reveal. In making this step one certainly must take seriously that African American men, themselves, often think about the contemporary street corner as a threatening site. Their own reaction to that space involves acknowledging the risks that are involved in spending significant time there (Anderson 1999; Venkatesh 2000; Young 2004). Thus, the reaction of outside observers, as well as many African American men, is that the modern urban street corner is no longer a safe site for the reconstitution of identities, but rather the cementing of devalued identities and images of these men (Oliver 2006; Payne 2006, 2008).

Rethinking the place of the street in the lives of Black men means reconsidering not only the inaccuracies of a street-centered focus, but how blinding such a focus has been for thinking about other dimensions of these men's lives. A part of the contemporary situation for these men, then, is the absence of public or institutionalized spaces for constructively working out and resolving tensions, perceived inadequacies, and self-misunderstandings about being fathers (and this is a problem that may be most effectively addressed by faith-based institutions, which, by their very nature, can provide such safe spaces and opportunities). They often find little support in formal organizational spaces, such as child welfare agencies or the legal system, where they (wrongly or rightly) perceive their interests to be suppressed by the attention given to women and children (Edin and Nelson 2013; Hamer 2001; Waller 2002). Hence, these men not only endure consistent social exposure as so-called "failed fathers" in their communities, but lack the means to express and resolve challenges to their capacity to serve as effective fathers because they recognize no formal or institutional outlets to do so (that is, unless they have access to social programs aimed at resolving these problems – and far too many low-income men lack such access).

What was easily ignored in emphases on low-income, urban-based African American men as representatives of the underclass is that such men construct senses of self and maintain identities that extend beyond what can be associated with the streets. One reason why the street-centered depiction is so problematic is that it became a public image associated with more urban-based men than it could appropriately be applied to. That image also prevented a more thorough and complex cultural portrait of these men from emerging such that the broader public often read them as wholly focused on hostility, threat, and anxiety. What this meant for low-income African American men who inhabited much of the urban space was that, even if they did not fully embrace this kind of depiction, often adapted styles of interaction and public engagement that provided measures of security and stability in communities from the 1970s to the 1990s were savaged by the proliferation of crack and increasing rates of crime. Hence, a more aggressive pursuit of how these men articulate meanings about the various features of their lives is in order.

Furthermore, the importance of securing safe spaces for discussing, questioning, and reconsidering healthy masculinity is counteracted by their living in spaces that are replete with the kinds of dangers, threats, and turbulence that have been well documented in social-scientific research on the contemporary urban community. Such space often demands that the young men who inhabit it take care to present and preserve public images of themselves as secure, vigilant, and truculent. The emotional consequence of maintaining these dispositions is that such men do not find value in, and therefore do not easily embrace, insecurity, hesitancy, and timidity as parts of their public persona. However, the very experience of coming into manhood is riddled with various emotional dynamics that require physical and emotional space for such considerations.

Without having the social space to approach, consider, and resolve or manage the tensions associated with masculinity (and when living in communities and households where there is limited, if any, access to the material resources that are associated with successfully engaging that role), there is ample opportunity for these men to react toward their partners, children, or other people in ways that further threaten their capacity to function. Hence, the opportunity to talk about and act on their concerns, anxieties, and insecurities, especially with other men of the same status and condition, is the first of many steps to take.

Concern rests not in how males manage social interaction in public spaces but rather in how to devise means and measures to assess any individual and collective emotional impact of consistent subjection to character assassination. The existence of character assassination may not result in any explicit impingement upon individual behavior or conduct. However, the extreme surveillance of and critical social judgment made about the conduct, action, or disposition exemplified by Black males may be causal factors for a range of unhealthy emotional and physical states of being.

We must acknowledge that they maintain outlooks and attitudes that are masked by the public sentiment about them. Accordingly, a unique vantage point that offers much virtue is looking at how Black males assess the American Dream. We must learn to believe that Black men believe in the American Dream. Yet, we must learn precisely how they construct their commitments to it (around family, community, identity, and employment). The effort is a core matter at the heart of investigations of their interior thinking. Yet it cannot easily be discerned from observation or survey-based inquiry. Returning again to the examples provided in previous chapters, we see that observing Smittie's behavior on the street corner with the young men who threatened him in no way reveals how much he took into account what the potential consequences of his actions would be and how he felt about his behavior. What he actually did to defend himself at the time was not consistent with his understanding and moral vision of the situation. Furthermore, the contemporary lifestyles of Blue the mover and the assistant pastor in no way revealed who they were in their pasts. Yet their pasts consistently stayed in their heads and served as an impetus for their more current everyday behavior.

When focused on behavior at the expense of a broader and more complete portrait of Black males, it becomes harder for others to fully absorb the depth of the tribulations that such people face and how much value is placed on Black boys living long enough to become young men. Indeed, the movement from childhood to manhood, itself, can be better understood as a hope and aspiration rather than a normal process. Becoming a man is an achievement that is not taken for granted in many struggling African American families. That case was made in the widely and critically acclaimed documentary *Hoop Dreams*, which was a hugely successful endeavor that grossed more than $11 million worldwide (1994). This documentary provided insight into the lives of two young Black boys as they moved from talented basketball-playing middle-school youth to their early college years. Neither came close to playing in the NBA (National Basketball Association), but the film tells a compelling account of how social relations, human capital, community structure, and luck and misfortune come together in the lives of two young Black men aspiring to fulfill their dreams.

In what would be an easily overlooked segment of the documentary for sports enthusiasts, the mother of one of the boys, Arthur Agee, is baking a cake in celebration of Arthur's upcoming 18th birthday. As she talks about him, she mentions that an 18th birthday is a big deal. It is such a big deal, she explains, not simply because it is an indication of her son becoming a man, but also because it is a birthday that is not guaranteed for many young African American males. She is preparing to celebrate him, in large part, because he soon will survive to become 18 years of age. When taking this kind of orientation into account, one must reconsider the unique ways in which life is valued and managed by young Black men who are subjected to economic constraint and disadvantage.

Too often, the flawed understanding of how these individuals assess the American Dream is that their visions are tied to the social worlds of professional athletics or Hip Hop culture. However, the American Dream for Black males is not all about a desire to live the fast life because the effort of such males to think only for today is a reality precisely if they cannot imagine a coherent tomorrow. Immediate gratification can be understood, then, as not resulting from an inability to defer to the future but an inability to embrace the notion that a future is even attainable.

To be sure, the challenge of embracing that notion does not mean that Black males simplistically commit to fatalism. Thus, an effort to demystify the character of Black males must first involve acknowledging that fatalism is an incomplete conceptual scheme for encapsulating the social outlooks of the racialized poor (Rios 2011; Venkatesh 2000, 2006; Young 2004). These studies and others (Fergus et al. 2014; Noguera 2008; Wilson 1996; Young 2004) indicate that Black males do not necessarily reject mainstream institutional spheres such as schooling but rather have negative experiences with individuals in these spheres. The result is that they face problems with *their encounters with* schools, employers, and legal authorities such as the police, but not with schooling, employment, or the institution of law in a general sense. Research reveals that such males do value schools, jobs, and family; yet they struggle with their personal experiences in each of these and other domains (Lewis-McCoy 2014; Noguera 2008; Venkatesh 2006; Wilson 1992; Young 2004). Hence, it is too simplistic to regard this population as engulfed in thinking that the world is against them and that they react with aggression and hostility because they believe there is nothing that they can do to change these conditions.

A renewed vision of Black men also includes a more thorough understanding of their capacity for transformation. Men like Blue, Chris, Smittie, and Milton, and the assistant pastor of the church that hosted me for my evening lecture, are all examples of men who have transformed. Other Black males have done so even if they have not been recognized for doing so. For instance, researchers have noted that Black fathers have engaged in nurturing roles for several decades, as their emotive and caretaking contributions have been vital to fulfilling family needs (Hamer 2001). This is particularly true of low-income biological fathers and social fathers who provide extended kin care for family members. For instance, Hamer (2001) finds that low-income nonresident fathers prioritize role modeling and caregiving when they discuss their contributions to their children's lives. Interestingly, much of the public conversation regarding "new fatherhood" and paternal responsibility focuses on precisely this kind of fathering within the married, nuclear-family context. But this focus on nuclear families limits our understanding of the myriad ways Black men practice expanded fatherhood. Again, we have limited knowledge and understanding of married, heterosexual Black fathers' experiences, particularly ones who are not low-income. Research gaps such as these may account for why Black fathers, in addition to still being problematized as in "crisis," have not been held up as, in fact, exemplars of engaged fathering.

* * * * *

Every tradition of inquiry on Black people, whether focused on men or women, includes some notion of what constitutes a healthy Black individual, and those notions change over time. My investigations of the early (and later) traditions of Black sociological thought were designed to explore what notions of healthy or positive Blackness were promoted and embraced over time and why (Young and Deskins 2001). I pursue this work so that, in my own efforts to make sense of contemporary Black men and Black masculinity, my work is informed by the idea that these efforts are situated in space and time, and thus susceptible to being re-thought and reconfigured in light of later social, political, and intellectual developments. The aim is to change the nature of the conversation about Black men, to foster new understandings of agency as it pertains to the case of Black men, and to bring to public attention various questions about the culture, identity, and public representation of such males. Accordingly, a renewed vision of Black men must also include space for depictions that allow for more than the normatively heterosexual imagery that has rather problematically stood the test of time as the only normative framework for such men (Drake 2016; Neal 2013).

The long-standing belief that the social worlds of African American males is so distant from those of other Americans is a legacy of the vision of the inner-city as an "other" kind of place that is not a part of "our" community. We must adhere to and advance the notion that Black males share membership in our national community. Black men have not rejected society as much as we have rejected them from full membership in society. We have done so because it appears to be easy to get along without them – socially and economically, if not culturally. Essentially, we must unlearn what we think we know about them and be prepared to think anew.

The ensuing challenge for researchers and interested parties, then, is to re-envision black males as complex human beings – a mixture of socially defined positive and negative attributes, much like other people – rather than wholly unworthy. It means embracing a vision of them as adherents to the same cultural schemas that apply to many Americans – as committed to the value of family, education, employment, and socioeconomic opportunity – even if actions sometimes surface due to the denial of the capacity to access these desires and outcomes. It means that the existence of Black males in trouble or who are troubling should not be the bedrock for interpreting the character and dispositions of all such males, nor should it be the basis for a default depiction of Black males as inherently flawed people, where the stereotypical portrait looms large. For the sake of Black males, the effects of their character assassination mandates further, more intense, and more specific forms of study. However, the public acknowledgment and acceptance of an alternative image of Black males and Black masculinity requires work, and a part of this work requires better apprehension of how and why Black males "feel" as they do and not just focusing on what it is that they do. A suspension (but certainly not abandoning) of moral judgments must give way to investing more immediately in understanding how and why these outcomes emerge.

The change necessary to allow Black men to prevail must take place in the arenas of policy and civil society, but also in the broader public consciousness as well. This effort must involve re-imaging these men not solely as sources and progenitors of social problems, but as people who are equipped to read and interpret much about who they are and why they made the behavioral choices that they did. These men are reflective, contemplating individuals who are not simply viscerally reacting in opposition to a social world that they perceive to be hostile and uninviting. Surely, they are complicated people, but not so much because they inspire intrigue over why they seemingly commit so much crime, or engage in so much violence, or seem so detached from and uninterested in their children. What is complicated about these men, I submit, is that they maintain a stronger moral and cognitive fiber than is often attributed to them. They possess a capacity to realize the effects of their actions, and construct judgments about them. They do so to an extent far beyond what has been implied in much of the contemporary public debate about them. Consequently, if Black men are to prevail in modern society, they must be more fully accepted as members of civil society. They must be seen not solely as people in need of intervention and correctives, but as people capable of participating with others in the improvement of their social position and correcting the problems they face – some of which is really a problem that others have with them and that needs to be addressed head on with courage and conviction.

Abbasi, Waseem. 2017. "Convictions are Rare for Police Officers in Police Shootings." *USA Today*, June 17. Retrieved on July 6, 2017, from https://www.usatoday.com/story/news/nation/2017/06/17/convictions-rare-officers-police-shootings/102947548

Abrahams, R.D. 1964. *Deep Down in the Jungle*, rev. edn. Chicago, IL: Aldine.

Alcindor, Y. 2012. "Trayvon Martin: Typical Teen or Troublemaker?" *USA Today*, December 11.

Alcindor, Y., Bello, M., & Madhani, A. 2014. "Chief: Officer Noticed Brown Carrying Suspected Stolen Cigars." *USA Today*, August 15.

Alvarez, L. 2013. "Defense in Trayvon Martin Case Raises Questions About the Victim's Character." *The New York Times*, May 23.

American Lung Association. 2007. *Too Many Cases, Too Many Deaths: Lung Cancer in African Americans*. Washington, DC: American Lung Association.

Anderson, E. 1989. "Sex Codes and Family Life Among Poor Inner-City Youth." *The ANNALS of the Academy of Political and Social Science*, 501: 59–78.

Anderson, E. 1990. *Streetwise: Race, Class, and Change in an Urban Community*. Chicago, IL: University of Chicago Press.

Anderson, E. 1999. *Code of the Street: Decency, Violence, and the Moral Life of the Inner City*. New York: Norton.

Aponte, R. 1990. "Definitions of the Underclass: A Critical Analysis." In H. Gans (ed.) *Sociology in America*. Newbury Park, CA: Sage.

References

Auletta, K. 1982. *The Underclass*. New York: Random House.

Berger, B. 1960. *Working-Class Suburb: A Study of Auto Workers in Suburbia*. Berkeley, CA: University of California Press.

Billson, J.M. 1996. *Pathways to Manhood: Young Black Males' Struggle for Identity*. New Brunswick, NJ: Transaction.

BlackDemographics.com. 2013. *The African American Population Report*, 1st edn. Available at: BlackDemographics.com

Bordua, D.J. 1961. "Delinquent Subcultures: Sociological Interpretations of Gang Delinquency." *The ANNALS of the American Academy of Political and Social Science*, 228: 120–36.

Bouie, J. 2017. "The Cloak of Fear." *Slate*, June 23. Retrieved on July 6, 2017, from http://www.slate.com/articles/news_and_politics/politics/2017/06/why_fear_was_a_viable_defense_for_killing_philando_castile.html

Bourgois, P. 1995. *In Search of Respect: Selling Crack in El Barrio*. New York: Cambridge University Press.

Bureau of Justice Statistics. 2010. *Prison Inmates at Midyear 2009 – Statistical Tables*. Washington, DC.

Bureau of Justice Statistics. 2015. *National Prisoner Statistics*. Washington, DC.

Burns, S. 2011. *The Central Park Five: A Chronicle of a City Wilding*. New York: Alfred Knopf.

Center for Economic and Policy Research. 2010. *Ex-Offenders and the Labor Market*. Washington, DC.

Centers for Disease Control and Prevention. 2016. *National Vital Statistics Reports*, 65(5).

Cloward, R.A., & Ohlin, L.E. 1960. *Delinquency and Opportunity: A Theory of Delinquent Gangs*. New York: Free Press.

Cohen, A.K., & Hodges, H.M. 1963. "Characteristics of the Lower Blue-Collars Class." *Social Problems*, 10(4): 303–34.

Collins, P.H. 2005. *Black Sexual Politics: African Americans, Gender, and the New Racism*. New York: Routledge.

References

Coser, L. 1965. "The Sociology of Poverty." *Social Problems*, 13(2): 140–8.

Drake, S. 2016. *When We Imagine Grace: Black Men and Subject Making*. Chicago, IL: University of Chicago Press.

Edin, K., & Nelson, T. 2013. *Doing the Best I Can: Fatherhood in the Inner City*. Berkeley, CA: University of California Press.

Farley, R., Danziger, S.H., & Holzer, H.J. 2000. *Detroit Divided*. New York: Russell Sage.

Fergus, E., Noguera, P., & Martin, M. 2014. *Schooling for Resilience: Improving the Life Trajectories of African American and Latino Males*. Cambridge, MA: Harvard Education Press.

Fitzsimmons, E. 2014. "12-Year-Old Boy Dies After Police in Cleveland Shoot Him." *The New York Times*, November 23.

Ford, K. 2008. "Gazing into the Distorted Looking Glass: Masculinity, Femininity, Appearance Ideals, and the Black Body." *Sociology Compass*, 2(3): 1096–114.

Ford, K. 2011. "Doing Fake Masculinity, Being Real Men: Present and Future Constructions of Self Among Black College Men." *Symbolic Interaction*, 34(1): 38–62.

Gans, H. 1962. *Urban Villagers*. New York: Free Press.

Gans, H. 1969. "Class in the Study of Poverty: An Approach to Anti-Poverty Research." In D.P. Moynihan (ed.) *On Understanding Poverty: Perspective from the Social Sciences*. New York: Basic Books.

Goffman, A. 2014. *On The Run: Fugitive Life in an American City*. Chicago, IL: University of Chicago Press.

Guerrero, E. 2012. *Framing Blackness: The African American Image in Film*. Philadelphia, PA: Temple University Press.

Hamer, J. 2001. *What It Means to be Daddy: Fatherhood for Black Men Living Away from their Children*. New York: Columbia University Press.

References

Hammond, W.P., & Mattis, J.S. 2005. "Being a Man About It: Manhood Meaning among African American Men." *Psychology of Men and Masculinity*, 6(2): 114–26.

Hammond, W.P., Chantala, K., Hastings, J.F., Neighbors, H.W., & Snowden, L. 2011. "Determinants of Usual Source of Care Disparities among African American and Caribbean Black Men: Findings from the National Survey of American Life." *Journal of Health Care for the Poor and Underserved*, 22: 157–75.

Hannerz, U. 1969. *Soulside: Inquiries into Ghetto Culture and Community*. New York: Columbia University Press.

Harding, D.J. 2010. *Living the Drama: Community, Conflict, and Culture among Inner-City Boys*. Chicago, IL: University of Chicago Press.

Hodgson, G. 1976. *America in Our Time: From World War II to Nixon – What Happened and Why*. Princeton, NJ: Princeton University Press.

Holzer, H.J., Offner, P., & Sorensen, E. 2005. "Declining Employment among Young Black Less-Educated Men: The Role of Incarceration and Child Support." *Journal of Policy Analysis and Management*, 24(2): 329–50.

Hunter, A.G., & Davis, J.E. 1992. "Constructing Gender: An Exploration of Afro-American Men's Conceptualization of Manhood." *Gender and Society*, 6(3): 464–79.

Husband, A. 2015. "CNN Describes Freddie Gray as 'Son of an Illiterate Heroin Addict,' Twitter Goes Nuts." *Mediaite*, November 30.

Institute of Education Sciences. 2013. "National Assessment of Educational Progress 2013 Mathematics and Reading Assessment." Washington, D.C.: National Center for Educational Statistics, US Department of Education.

Kaiser Family Foundation. 2006. *Race, Ethnicity Health Care Fact Sheet*. Washington, DC.

Koven, M.J. 2010. *Blaxploitation Films*. Harpenden: Kamera Books.

103

References

Lewis, O. 1959. *Five Families: Mexican Case Studies in the Culture of Poverty*. New York: Basic Books.

Lewis, O. 1961. *The Children of Sanchez*. New York: Random House.

Lewis, O. 1966. *La Vida: A Puerto Rican Family in the Culture of Poverty, San Juan and New York*. New York: Random House.

Lewis-McCoy, R.L'Heureux. 2014. *Inequality in the Promised Land: Race, Resources and Suburban Schooling*. Stanford, CA: Stanford University Press.

Liebow, E. 1967. *Tally's Corner: A Study of Negro Streetcorner Men*. Boston, MA: Little, Brown.

Majors, R., & Billson, J.M. 1992. *Cool Pose: The Dilemmas of Black Manhood in America*. New York: Lexington Books.

Miller, W.B. 1958. "Lower Class Culture as a Generating Milieu of Gang Delinquency." *Journal of Social Issues*, 14(3): 5–19.

National Center for Health Statistics. 2007. *Health, United States, 2007: with Chartbook on Trends in the Health of Americans*. Hyatsville, MD: NCHS.

National Urban League. 2007. *The State of Black America: Portrait of the Black Male*. New York: Beckham Publication Group.

Neal, M.A. 2006. *New Black Man*. New York: Routledge.

Neal, M.A. 2013. *Looking for Leroy: Illegible Black Masculinities*. New York: New York University Press.

Noguera, P.A. 2008. *The Trouble with Black Boys and Other Reflections on Race, Equity, and the Future of Public Education*. New York: John Wiley & Sons.

O'Connor, A. 2001. *Poverty Knowledge: Social Science, Social Policy, and the Poor in Twentieth-Century U.S. History*. Princeton, NJ: Princeton University Press.

Office of Minority Health. 2008. *African American Profile*. Rockville, MD: OMH.

Oliver, W. 2006. "'The Streets:' An Alternative Black Male Socialization Institution." *Journal of Black Studies*, 36(6): 918–37.

References

Opportunity Agenda. 2012. *Social Science Literature Review: Media Representations and Impact on the Lives of Black Men and Boys.* Available at: http://www.racialequitytools.org/resourcefiles/Media-Impact-onLives-of-Black-Men-and-Boys-OppAgenda.pdf

Pager, D. 2007. *Marked: Race, Crime, and Finding Work in an Era of Mass Incarceration.* Chicago, IL: University of Chicago Press.

Pager, D., Western, B., & Bonikowski, B. 2009a. "Discrimination in a Low Wage Labor Market: A Field Experiment." *American Sociological Review*, 74(5): 777–99.

Pager, D., Western, B., & Sugie, N. 2009b. "Sequencing Disadvantage: Barriers to Employment Facing Young Black and White Men with Criminal Records." *The ANNALS of the American Academy of Political and Social Science*, 623: 195–213.

Payne, Y.A. 2006. "'A Gangster and a Gentleman:' How Street Life-Oriented, US-Born African Men Negotiate Issues of Survival in Relation to their Masculinity." *Men and Masculinities*, 8: 288–97.

Payne, Y.A. 2008. "'Street Life' as a Site of Resiliency: How Street Life-Oriented Black Men Frame Opportunity in the United States." *Journal of Black Psychology*, 34: 3–31.

Quadagno, J. 1994. *The Color of Welfare: How Racism Undermined the War on Poverty.* New York: Oxford University Press.

Quillian, L.G., & Pager, D. 2001. "Black Neighborhoods, Higher Crime? The Role of Racial Stereotypes in Evaluations of Neighborhood Crime." *American Journal of Sociology*, 107(3): 717–67.

Rainwater, L. 1970. *Behind Ghetto Walls: Black Families in a Federal Slum.* Chicago, IL: Aldine.

Ralph, L., & Chance, K. 2014. "Legacies of Fear: From Rodney King's Beating to Trayvon Martin's Death." *Transition*, 113: 137–43.

Redcross, C., Bloom, D., Jacobs, E., Manno, M., Muller-Ravett, S., Seefeldt, K., Yahner, J., Young, Jr., A.A., & Zweig, J. 2010. "Work After Prison: One-Year Findings from the Transitional Jobs Reentry

Demonstration." Indiana University-Bloomington: School of Public & Environmental Affairs Research Paper Series, No. 2011-03-04.

Riessman, F. 1962. *The Culturally Deprived Child*. New York: Harper.

Rios, V. 2011. *Punished: Policing the Lives of Black and Latino Boys*. New York: New York University Press.

Robles, F. 2012. "Multiple Suspensions Paint Complicated Portrait of Trayvon Martin." *The Miami Herald*, March 26.

Rodman, H. 1963. "The Lower-Class Value Stretch." *Social Forces*, 42(2): 205–15.

Russell-Brown, K. 2009. *The Color of Crime*, 2nd edn. New York: New York University Press.

Schott Foundation for Public Education. 2015. "Black Lives Matter: The Schott 50 State Report on Public Education and Black Males."

Schultz, D. 1969. *Coming Up Black: Patterns of Ghetto Socialization*. Englewood Cliffs, NJ: Prentice-Hall.

Sullivan, M.L. 1989. *Getting Paid: Youth, Crime, and Work in the Inner City*. Ithaca, NY: Cornell University Press.

Suttles, G. 1968. *The Social Order of the Slum*. Chicago, IL: University of Chicago Press.

Swisher, R.R., & Waller, M.R. 2008. "Confining Fatherhood: Incarceration and Paternal Involvement among Nonresident White, African American, and Latino Fathers." *Journal of Family Issues*, 29(8): 1067–88.

Tacopino, J. 2014. "Darren Wilson on Why He Shot Michael Brown." *New York Post*, November 25.

The Sentencing Project. 2013. "Report of The Sentencing Project to the United Nations Human Rights Committee Regarding Racial Disparities in the United States Criminal Justice System." Washington, DC.

Thrasher, Stephen W. 2017. "Police Hunt and Kill Black People Like Philano Castile. There's No Justice." *The Guardian*, June 19. Retrieved on July 6, 2017, from https://www.theguardian.com/commentisfree/2017/jun/19/philando-castille-police-violence-black-americans

References

US Census Bureau. 2012. *American Community Survey*. Washington, DC.

US Renal Data System. 2005. *USRDS 2005 Annual Data Report: Atlas of End-Stage Renal Disease in the United States*. Bethseda, MD: National Institutes of Health, National Institute of Diabetes and Digestive and Kidney Diseases.

Venkatesh, S.A. 2000. *American Project: The Rise and Fall of a Modern Ghetto*. Cambridge, MA: Harvard University Press.

Venkatesh, S.A. 2006. *Off the Books: The Underground Economy of the Urban Poor*. Cambridge, MA: Harvard University Press.

Wacquant, L. 2001. "Deadly Symbiosis: When Ghetto and Prison Meet and Mesh." *Punishment and Society*, 3: 95–133.

Wacquant, L. 2005. "Race as Civil Felony." *International Social Science Journal*, 57(183): 127–42.

Wacquant, L. 2010. "Class, Race, and Hyperincarceration in Revanchist America." *Daedalus*, 139: 74–90.

Waller, M. 2002. *My Baby's Father: Unmarried Parents and Paternal Responsibility*. Ithaca, NY: Cornell University Press.

Warner, D.F., & Hayward, M.D. 2006. "Early Life Origins of the Race Gap in Men's Mortality." *Journal of Health and Social Behavior*, 47(3): 209–26.

Western, B., & Wildeman, C. 2009. "The Black Family and Mass Incarceration." *The ANNALS of the American Academy of Political and Social Science*, 621: 221–42.

Whyte, W.F. 1943. *Street Corner Society: The Social Structure of an Italian Slum*. Chicago, IL: University of Chicago Press.

Williams, D.R. 2003. "The Health of Men: Structured Inequalities and Opportunities." *American Journal of Public Health*, 93(5): 724–31.

Williams, T. 1989. *Cocaine Kids: The Inside Story of a Teenage Drug Ring*. New York: Da Capo Press.

Wilson, W.J. 1987. *The Truly Disadvantaged: The Inner-City, the Underclass, and Public Policy*. Chicago, IL: University of Chicago Press.

References

Wilson, W.J. 1992. "The Plight of the Inner-City Black Male." *Proceedings of the American Philosophical Society*, 136(3): 320–5.

Wilson, W.J. 1996. *When Work Disappears: The World of the New Urban Poor*. New York: Knopf.

Wolfers, J., Leonhardt, D., & Quealy, K. 2015. "1.5 Million Missing Black Men." *The New York Times*, April 20.

Xanthos, C., Treadwell, H.M., & Holden, K.B. 2010. "Social Determinants of Health among African-American Men." *Journal of Men's Health*, 7(1): 11–19.

Young, Jr., A.A. 2000. "On the Outside Looking In: Low-Income Black Men's Conceptions of Work Opportunity and the 'Good Job.'" In S. Danziger & A.C. Lin (eds.) *Coping with Poverty: The Social Contexts of Neighborhood, Work, and Family in the African American Community*. Ann Arbor, MI: University of Michigan Press.

Young, Jr., A.A. 2004. *The Minds of Marginalized Black Men: Making Sense of Mobility, Opportunity, and Future Life Chances*. Princeton, NJ: Princeton University Press.

Young, Jr., A.A. 2006. "Low-Income Black Men on Work Opportunity, Work Resources, and Job Training Programs." In R. Mincy (ed.) *Black Males Left Behind*. Washington, DC: Urban Institute Press.

Young, Jr., A.A. 2007. "The Redeemed Old Head: Articulating a Sense of Public Self and Social Purpose." *Symbolic Interaction*, 30(3): 347–74.

Young, Jr., A.A. 2016. "Safe Spaces for Vulnerability: New Perspectives on African American Men and the Struggle to be Good Fathers." In L.M. Burton, D. Burton, S.M. McHale, V. King, & J. Van Hook (eds.) *Boys and Men in African American Families*. Cham: Springer.

Young, Jr., A.A. 2017. "The Character Assassination of Black Males: Some Consequences for Research in Public Health." In K. Bogard et al. (eds.) *Perspectives on Health Equity and Social Determinants of Health*. Washington, DC: National Academy of Medicine, pp. 101–15.

Young, Jr., A.A., & Deskins, Jr., D.R. 2001. "Early Traditions of African-American Sociological Thought." *Annual Review of Sociology*, 27: 445–77.

Index